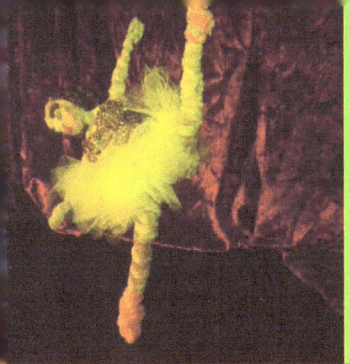
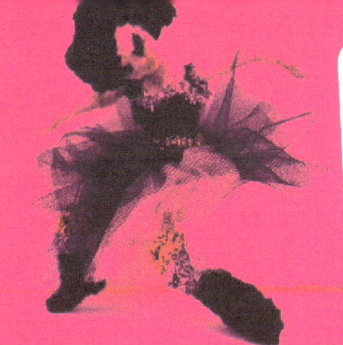

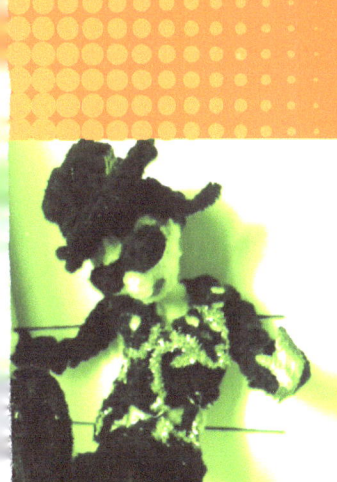
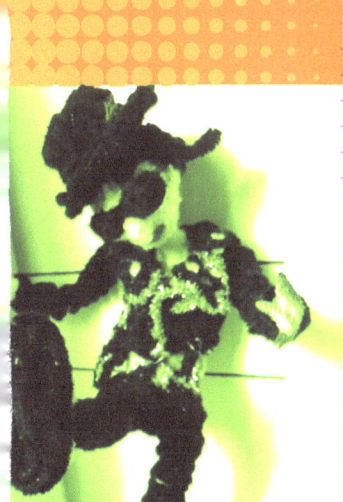

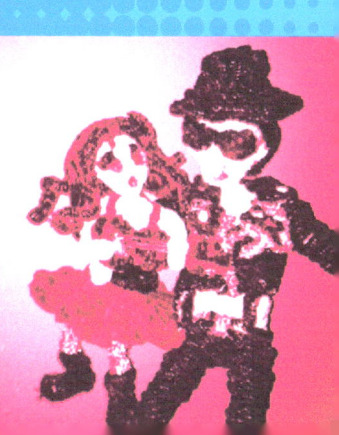

DANCE

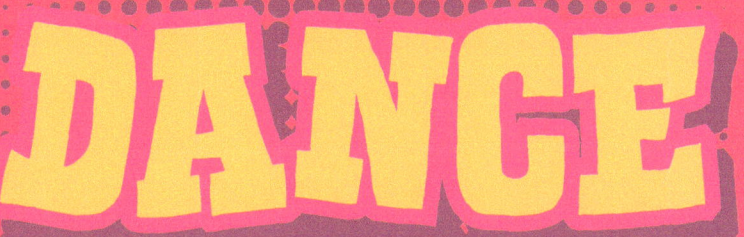
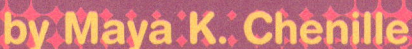

by Maya K. Chenille

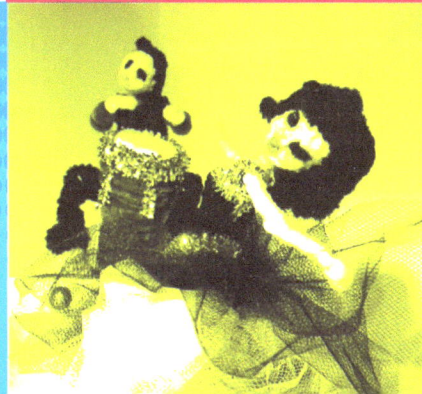

Special thanks to
Terry Sendgraff, Billy Burke, and Rosemary Valaire for all
they taught me as a dancer and as a human being.

Very special thanks to
Joe Turner (www.dragonjoe.com) for teaching
me the art of making dolls.

Photographs and 3D art by Maya K. Chenille
shoeboxcircus@gmail.com

art direction & design
jessee vidaurre / factotum design

I love to **dance.** If you asked me why, it would be hard to explain, but I promise to try.

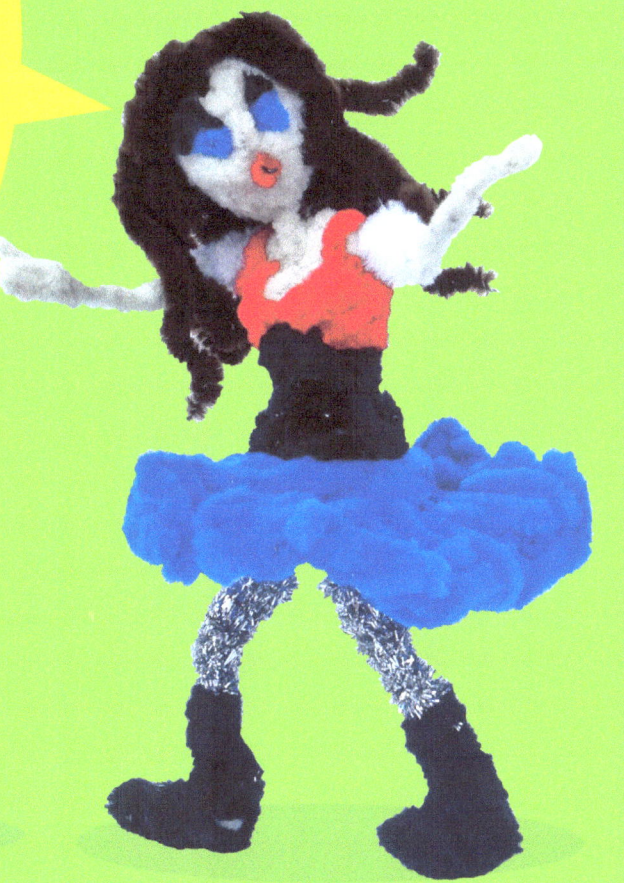

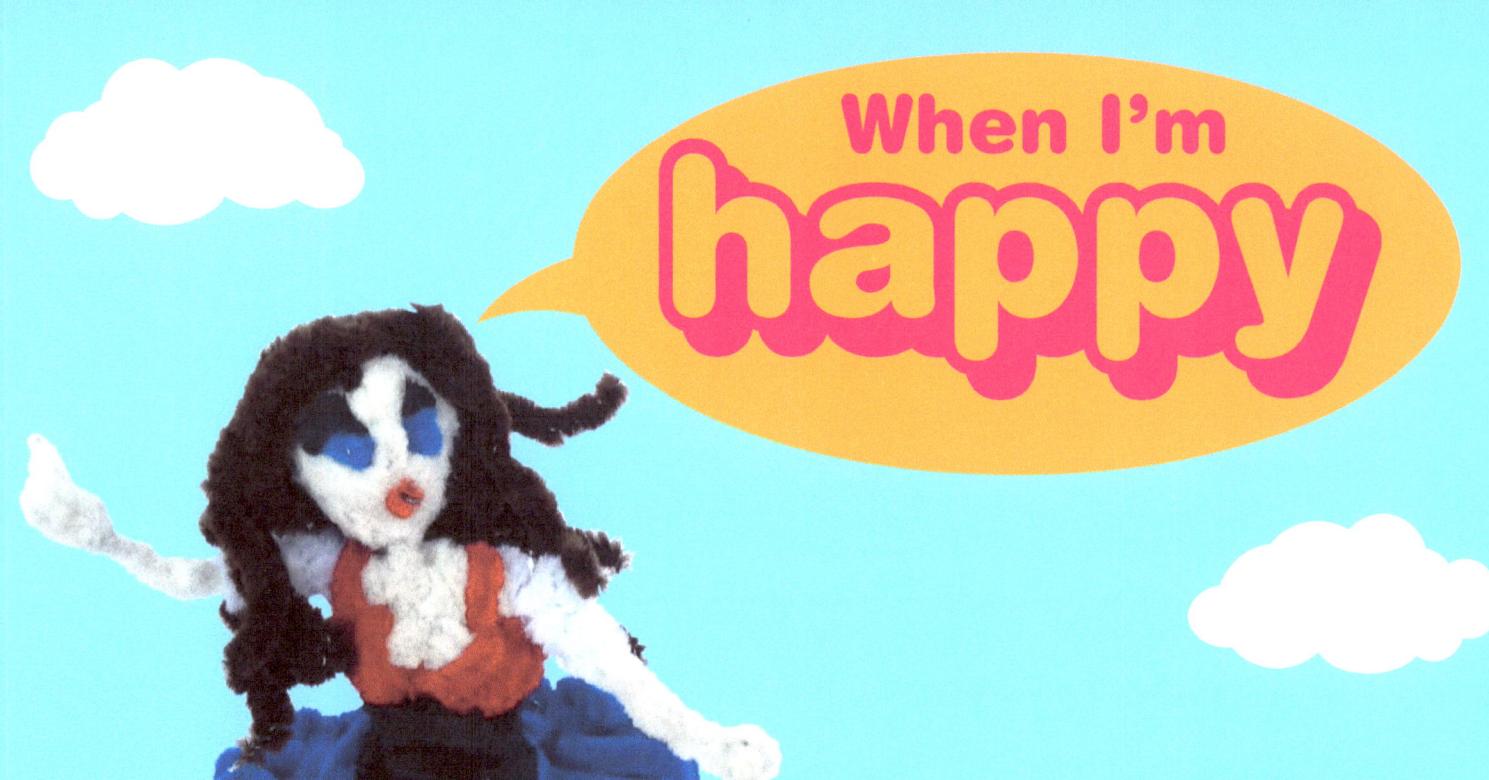

When I'm **happy**

I dance to **celebrate!**

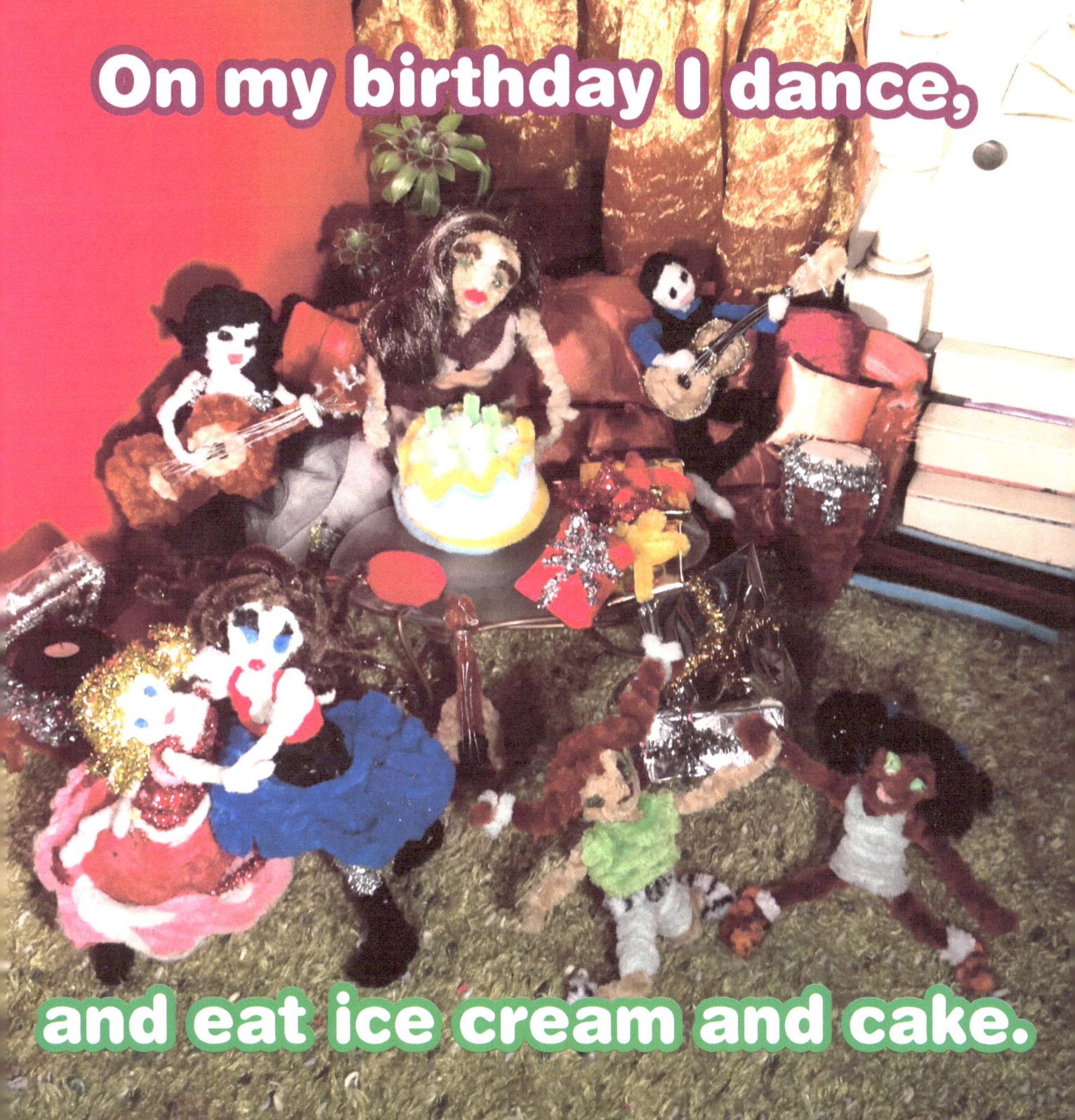

On my birthday I dance,

and eat ice cream and cake.

When I feel **angry**

I explode in my dance!

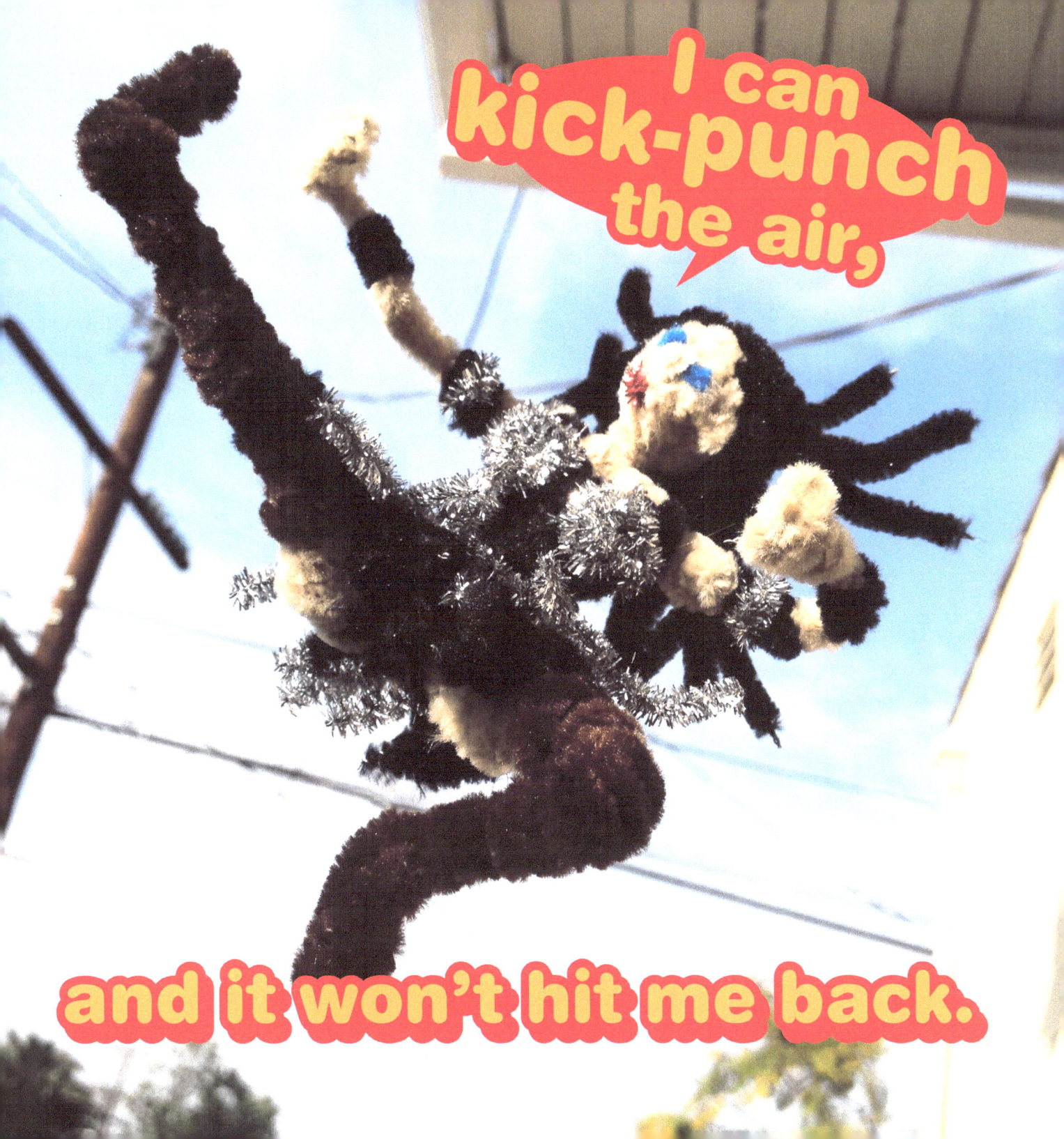

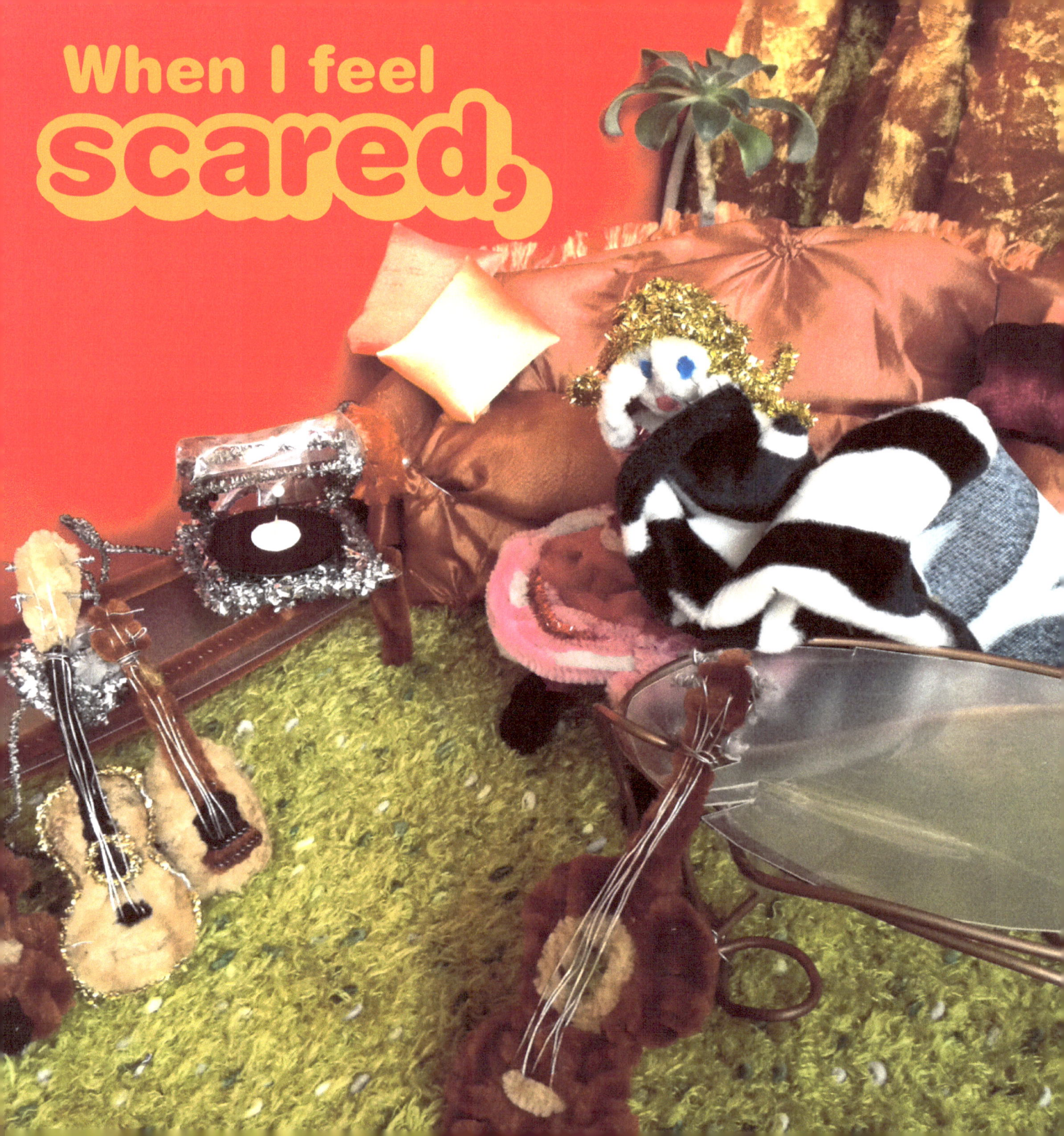

When I feel
scared,

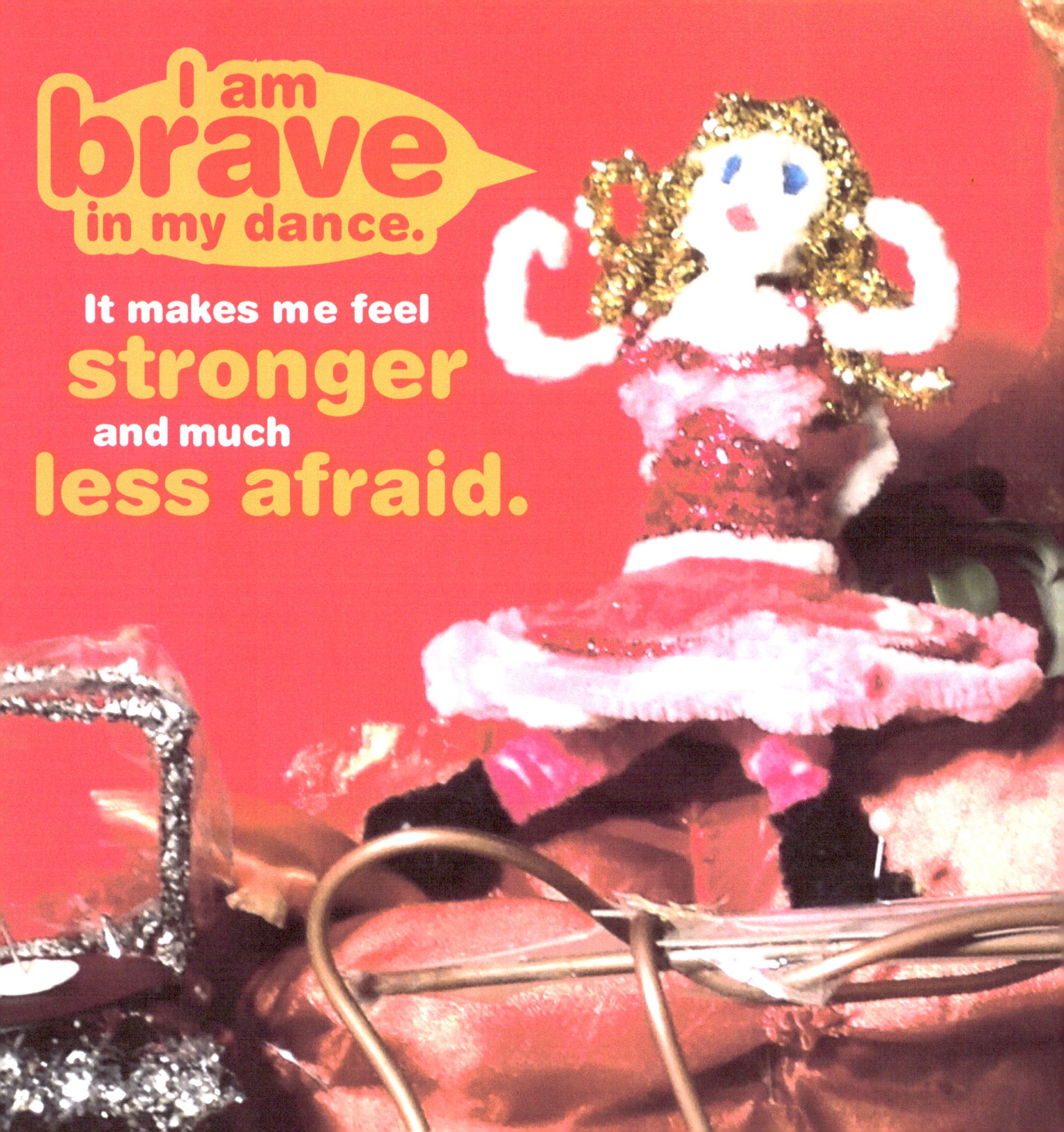

I am **brave** in my dance.

It makes me feel **stronger** and much **less afraid.**

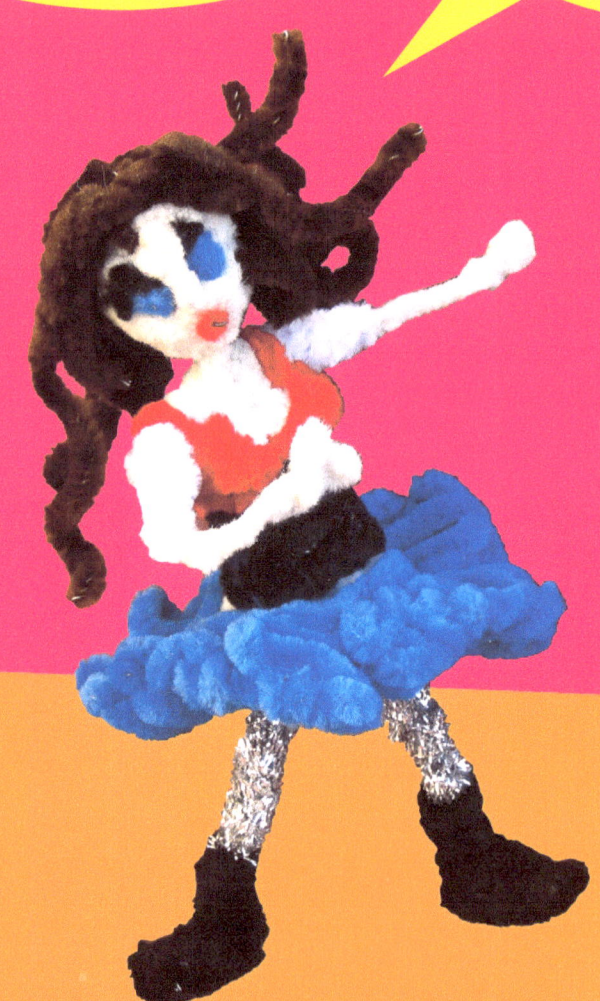

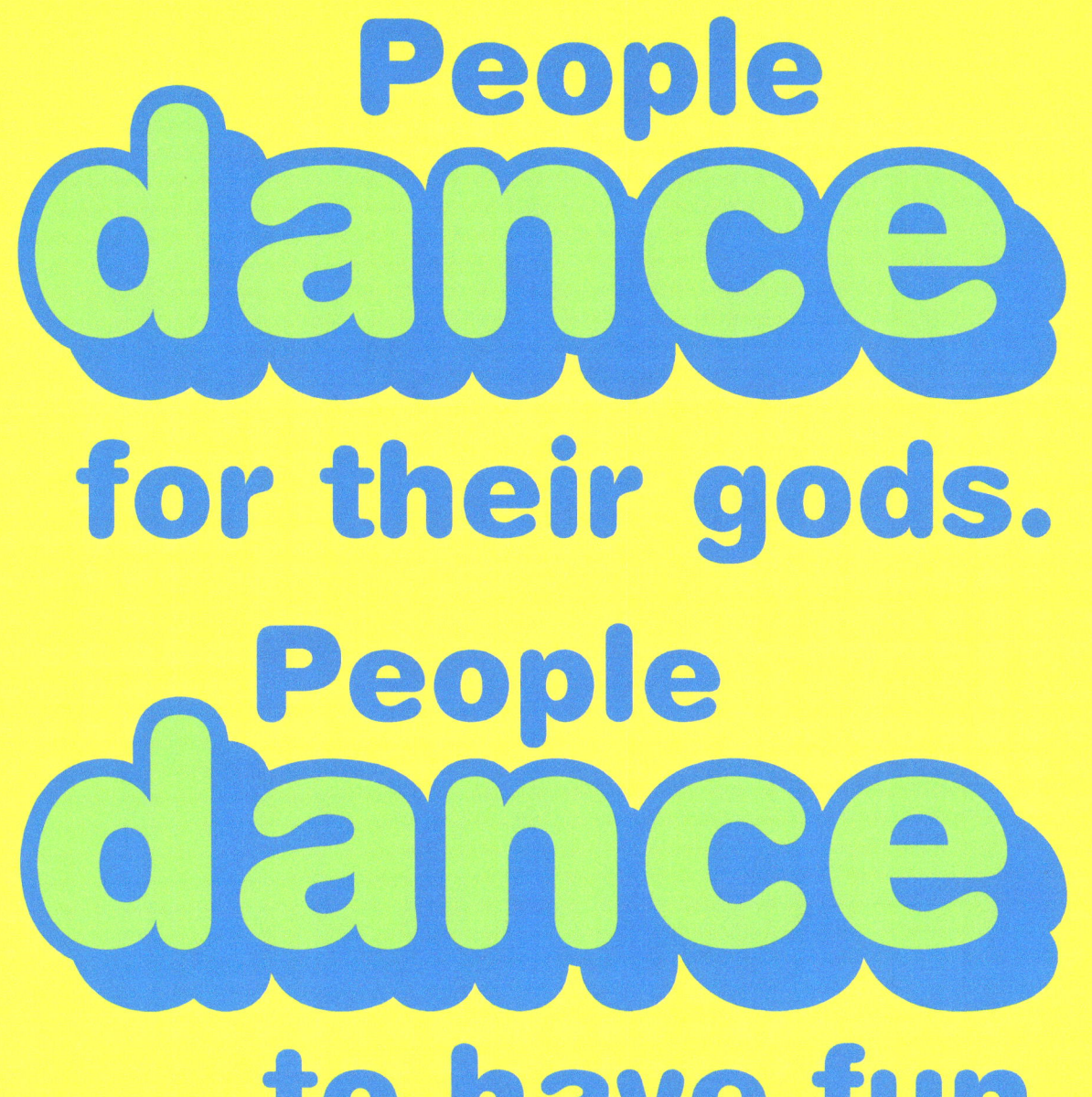

People dance for their gods. People dance to have fun.

People dance on the stage,

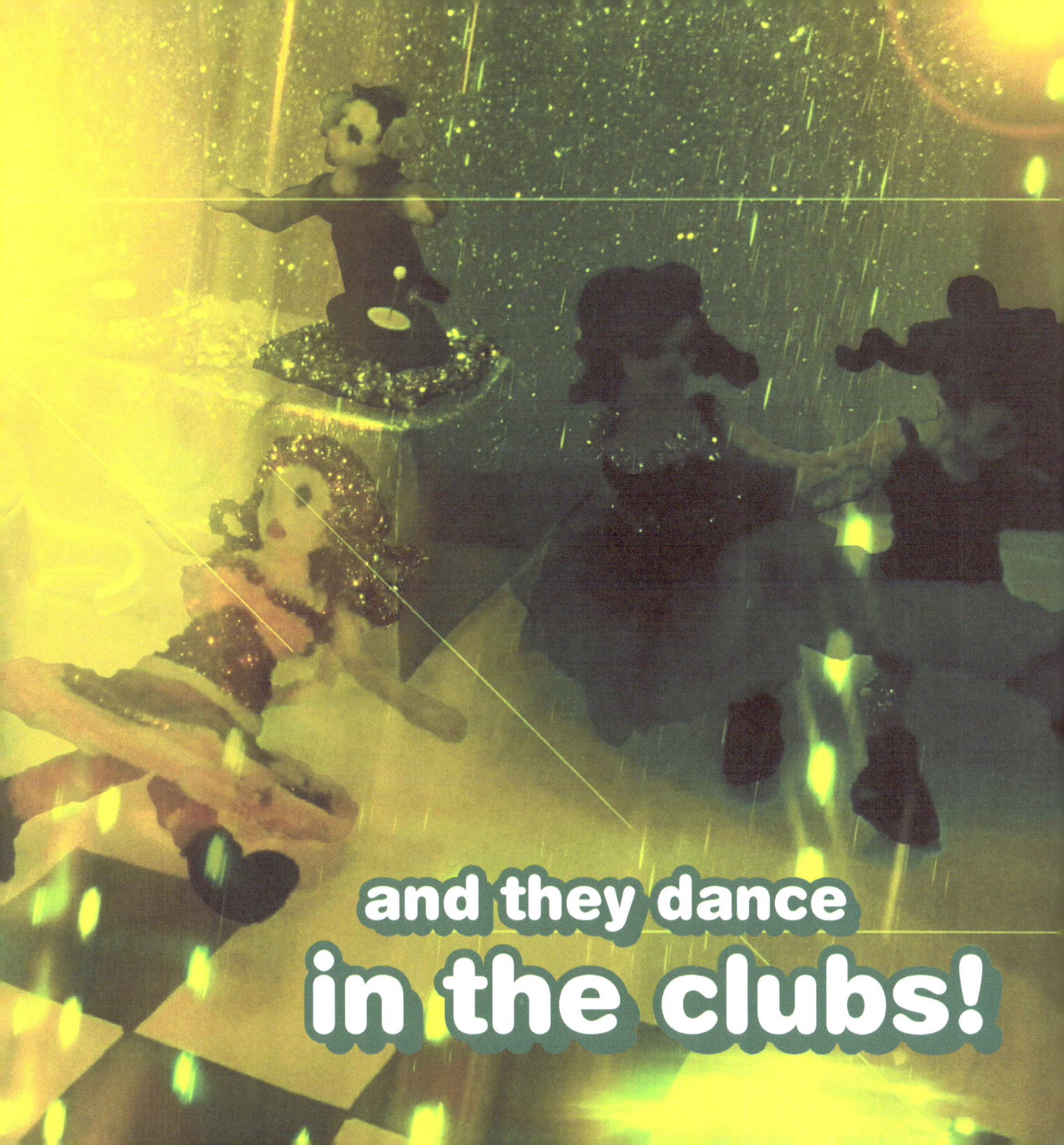

and they dance
in the clubs!

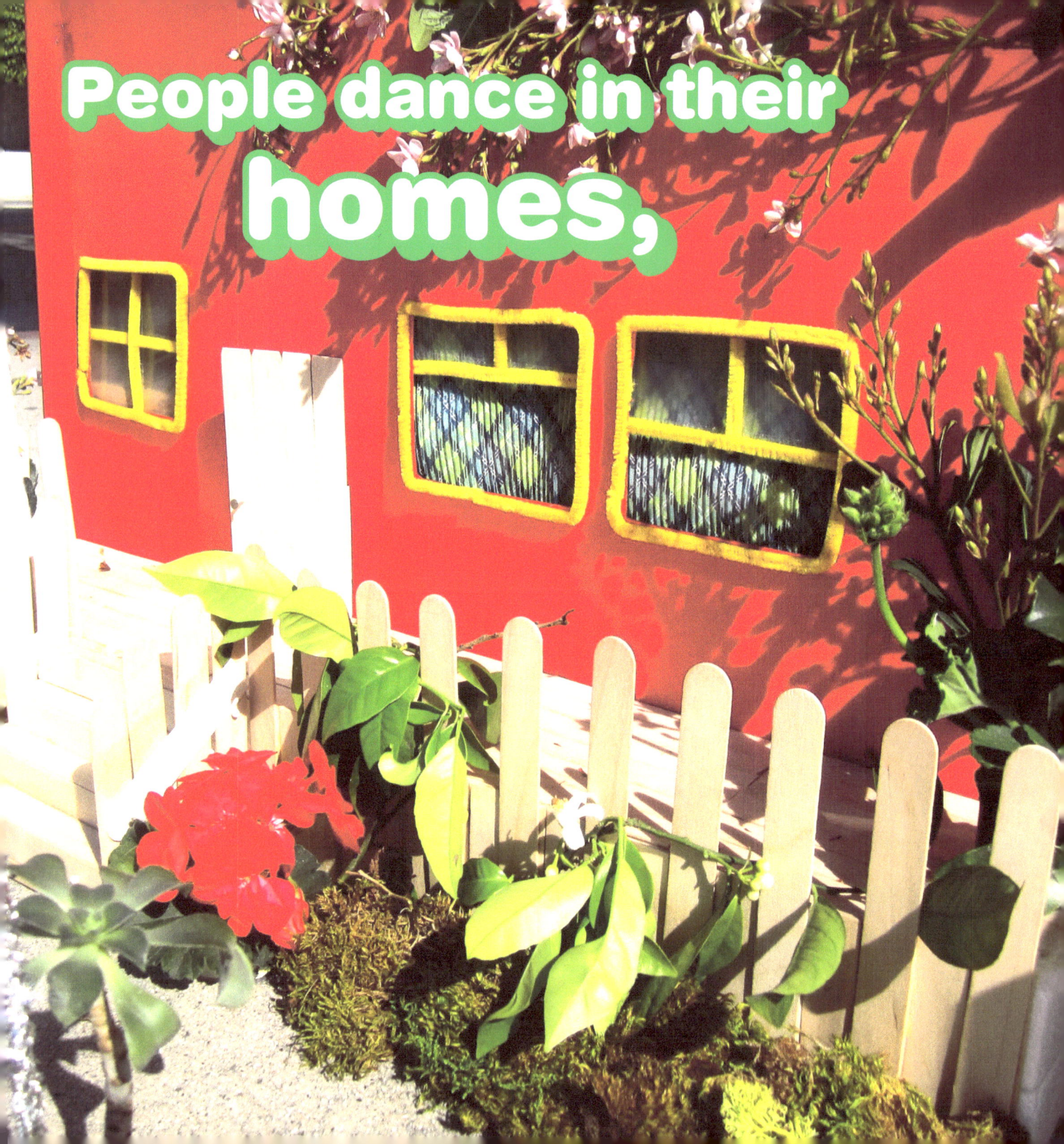

People dance in their
homes,

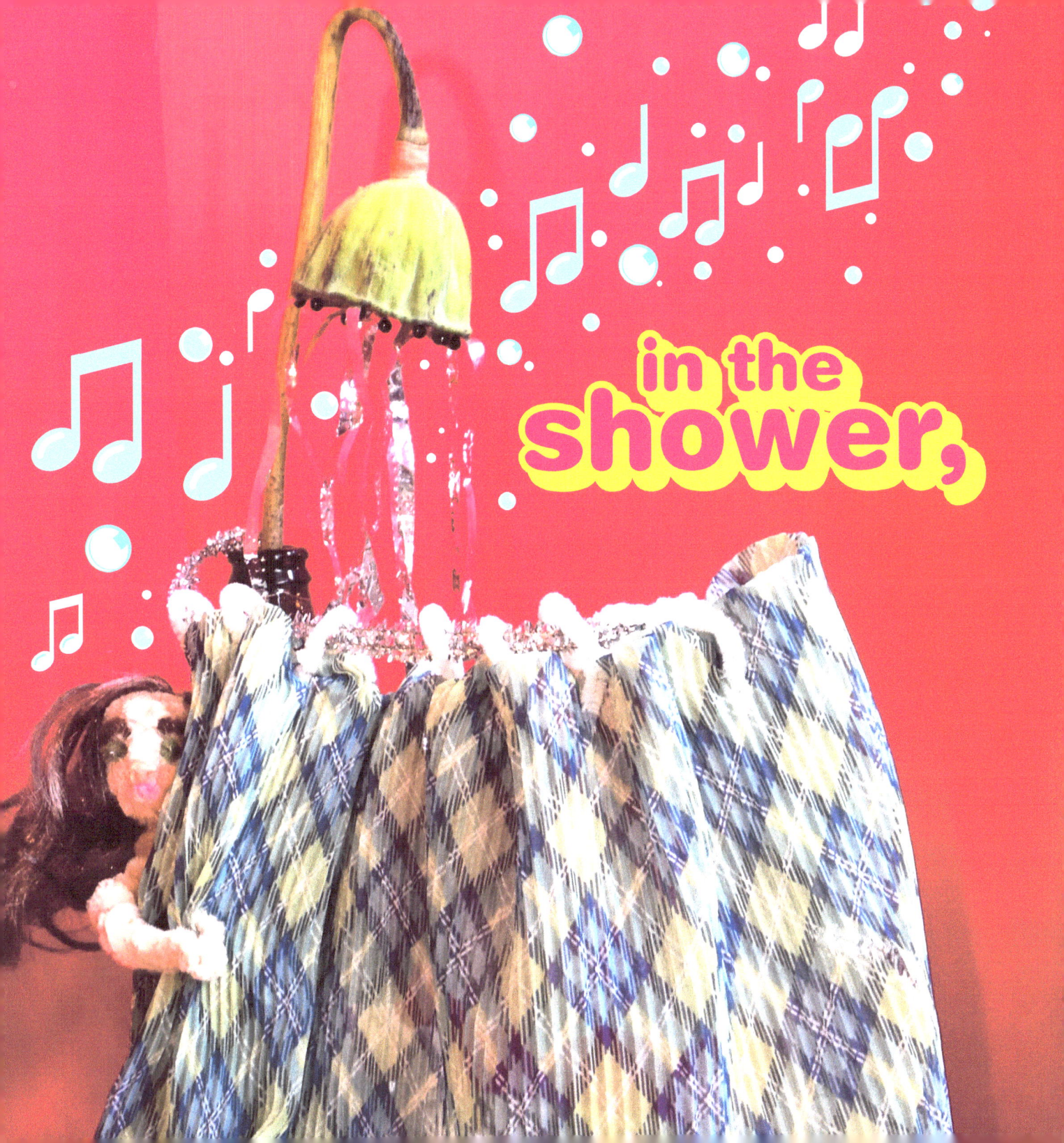

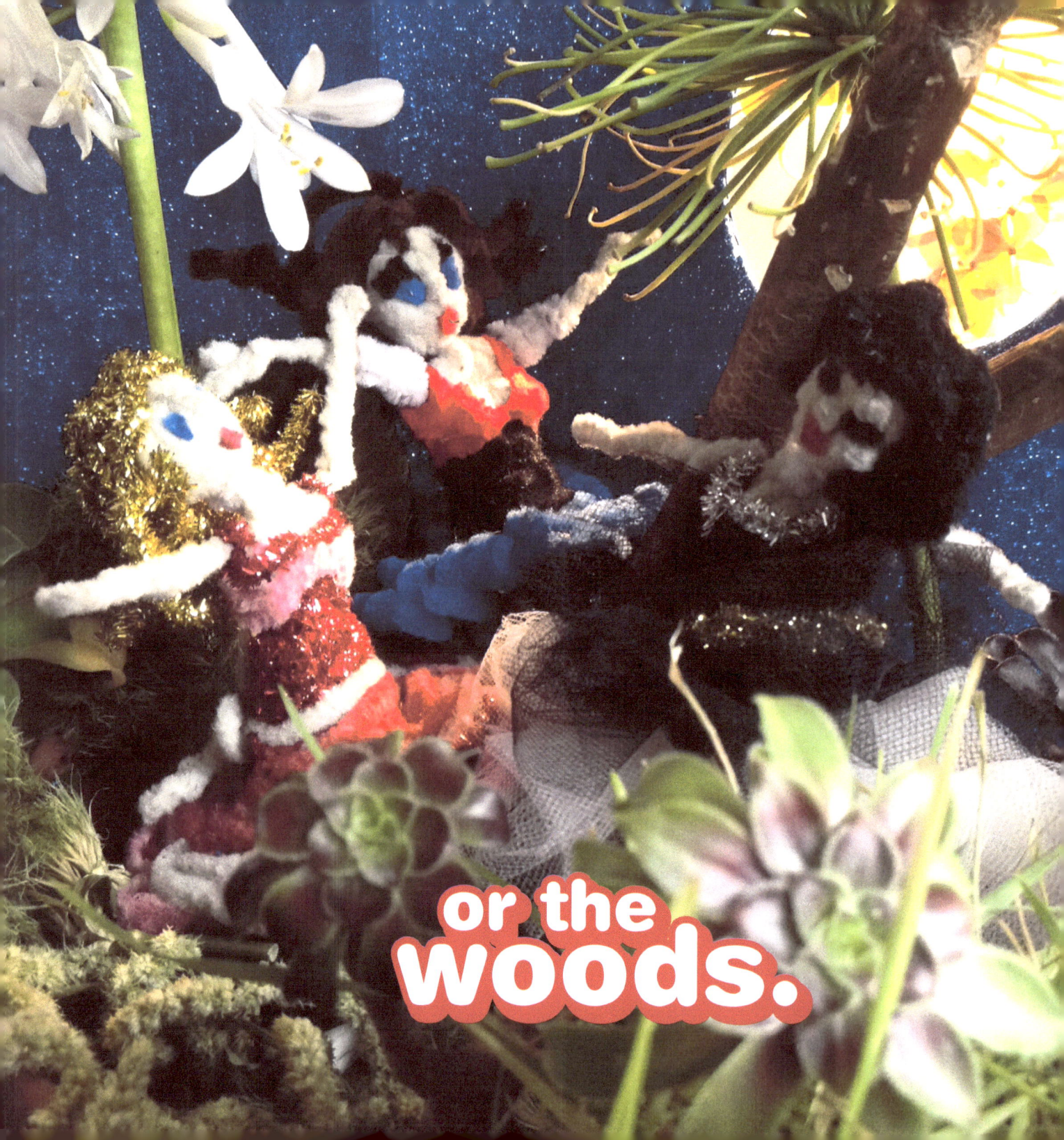

or the
woods.

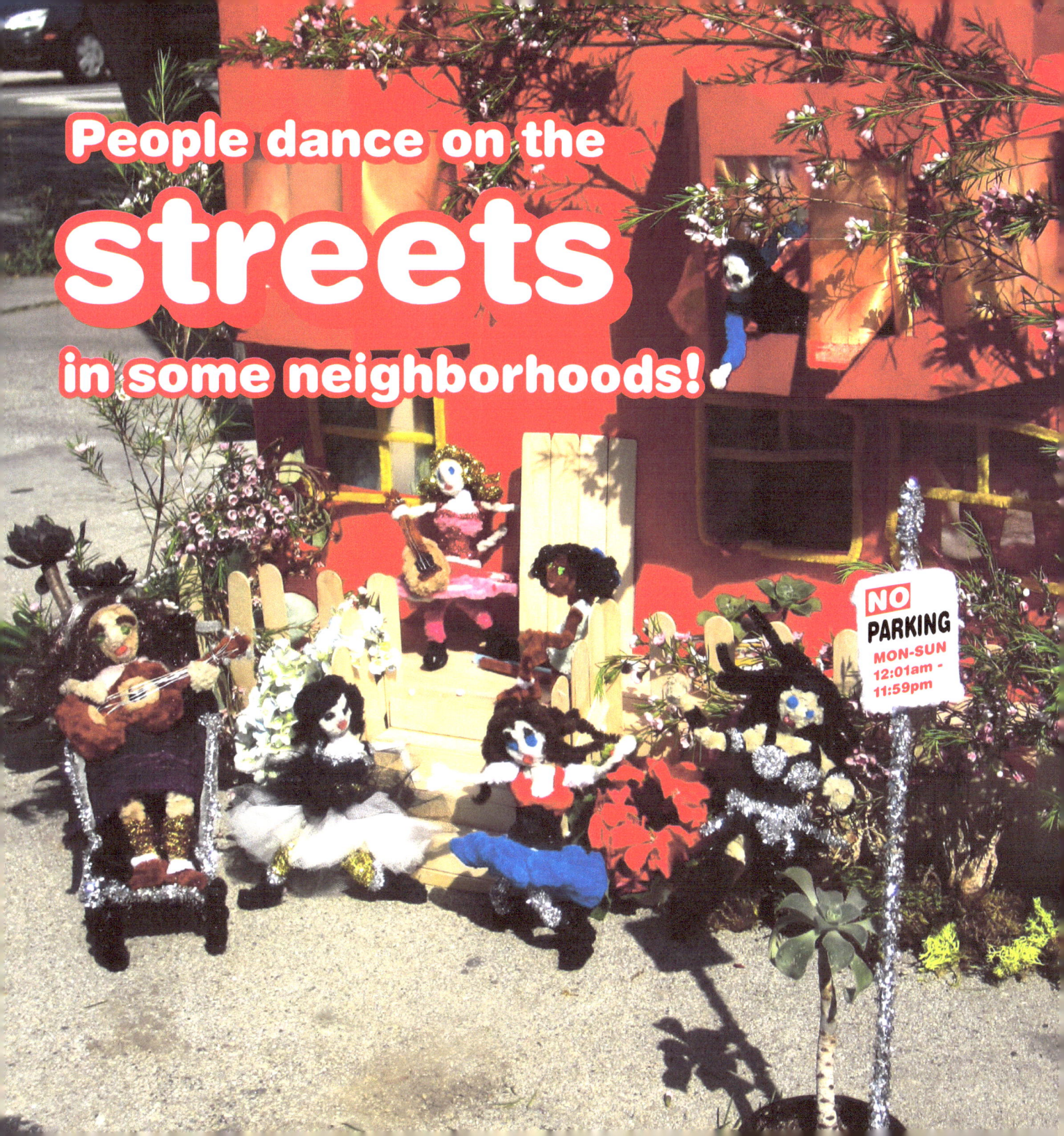

People dance on the **streets** in some neighborhoods!

NO PARKING MON-SUN 12:01am - 11:59pm

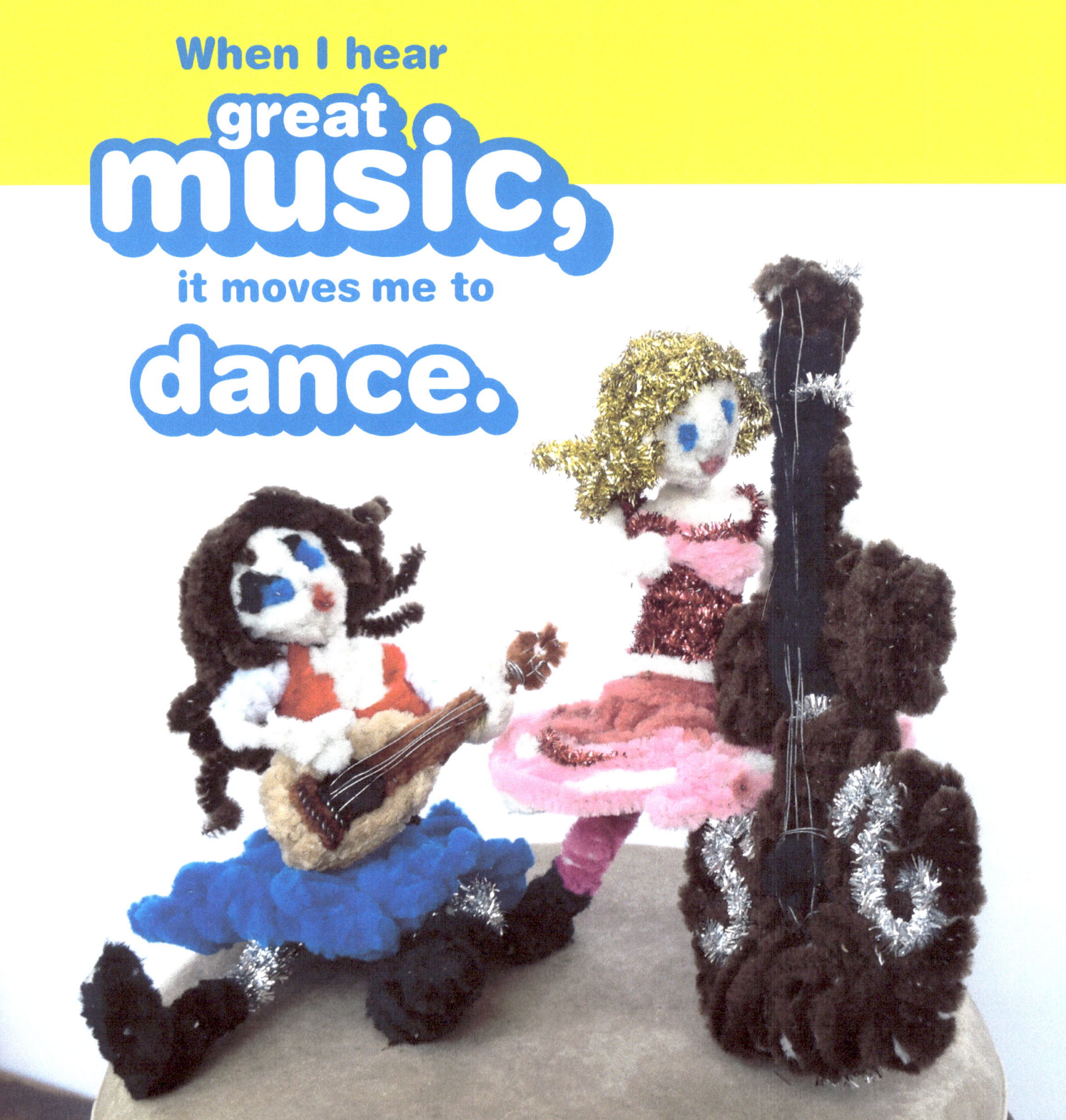

When I hear **great music,** it moves me to **dance.**

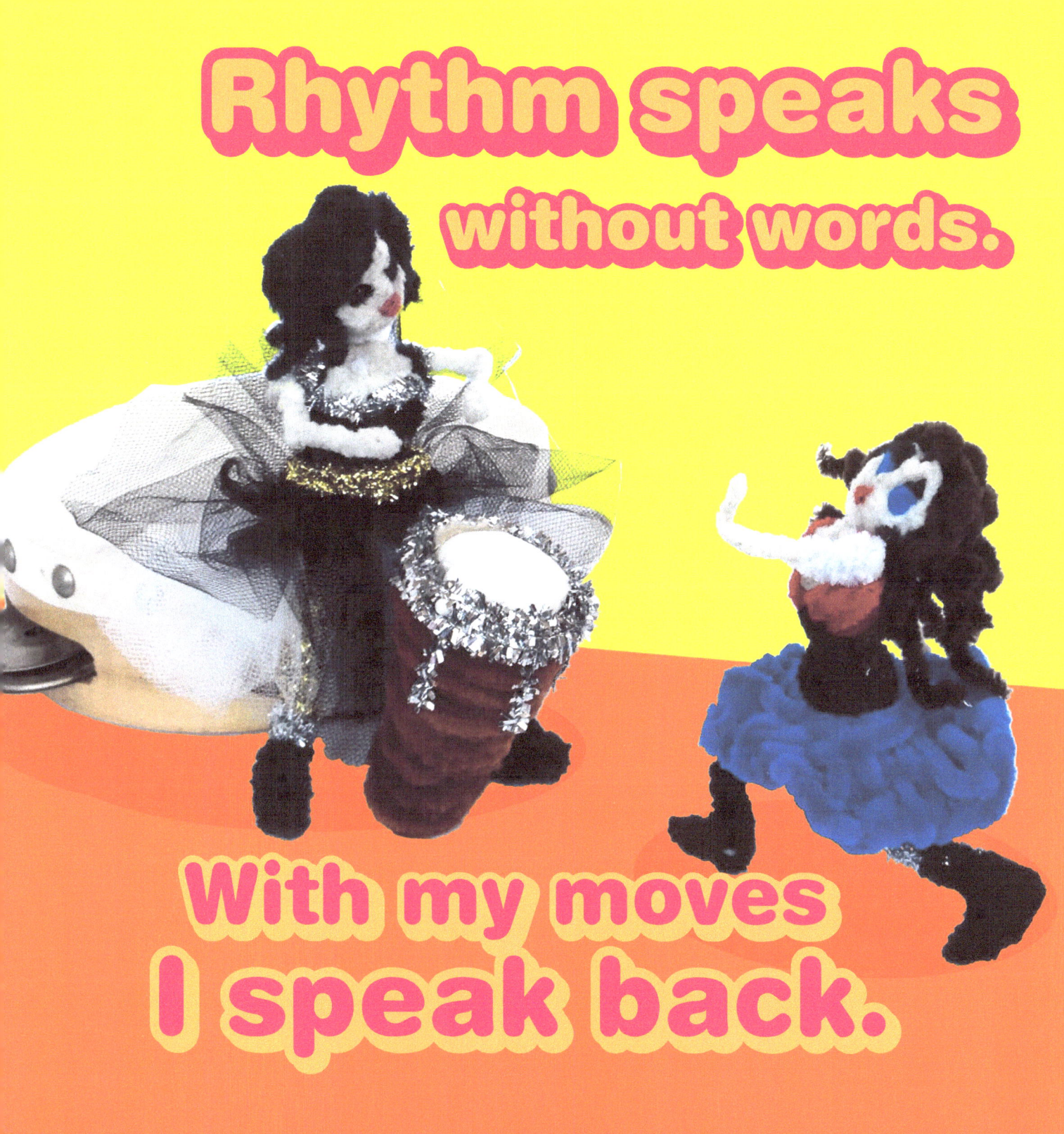

You can
leap, glide, or spin.
You can
skip, hop, or twirl.

It doesn't matter...

if you're a

boy

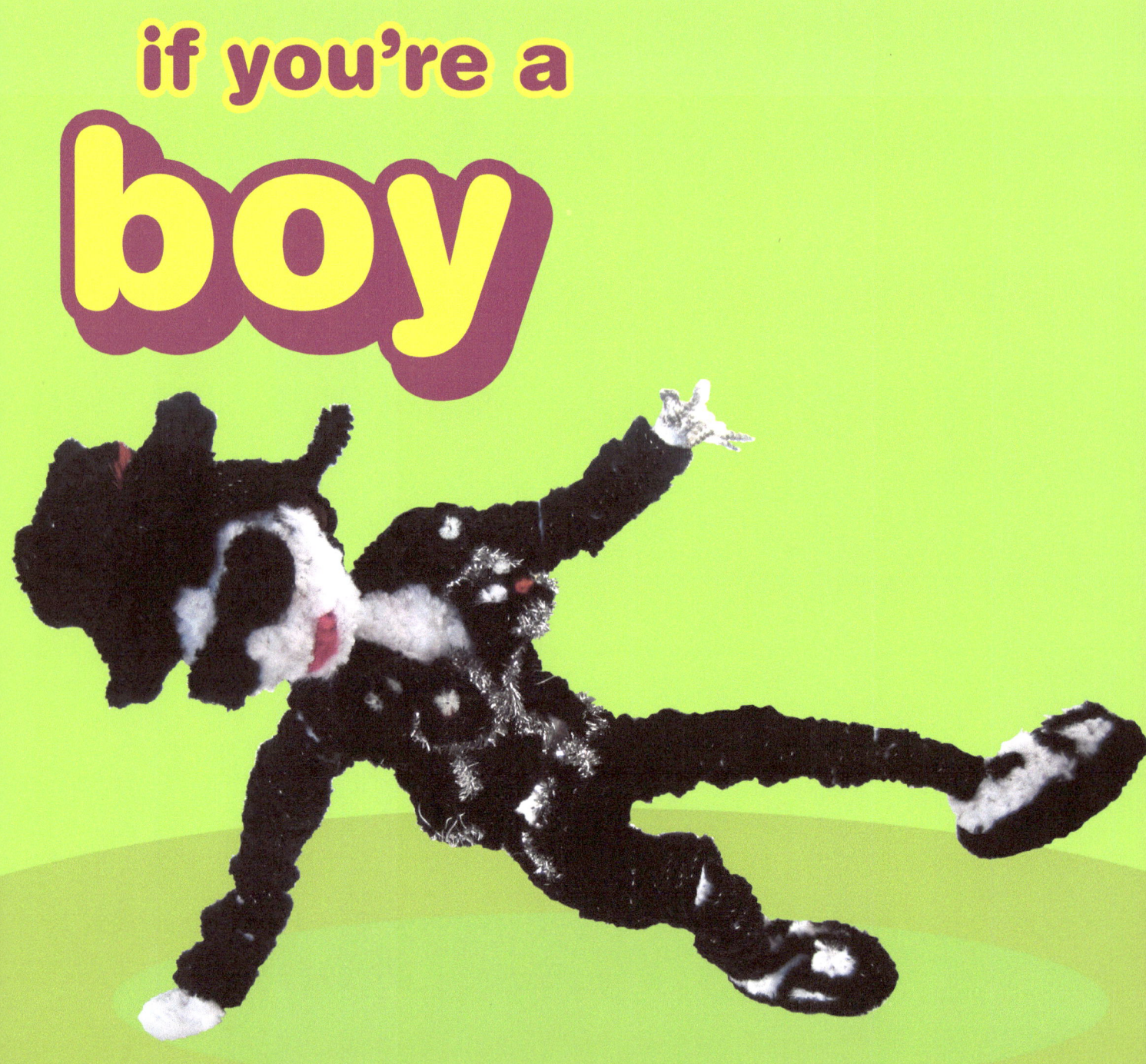

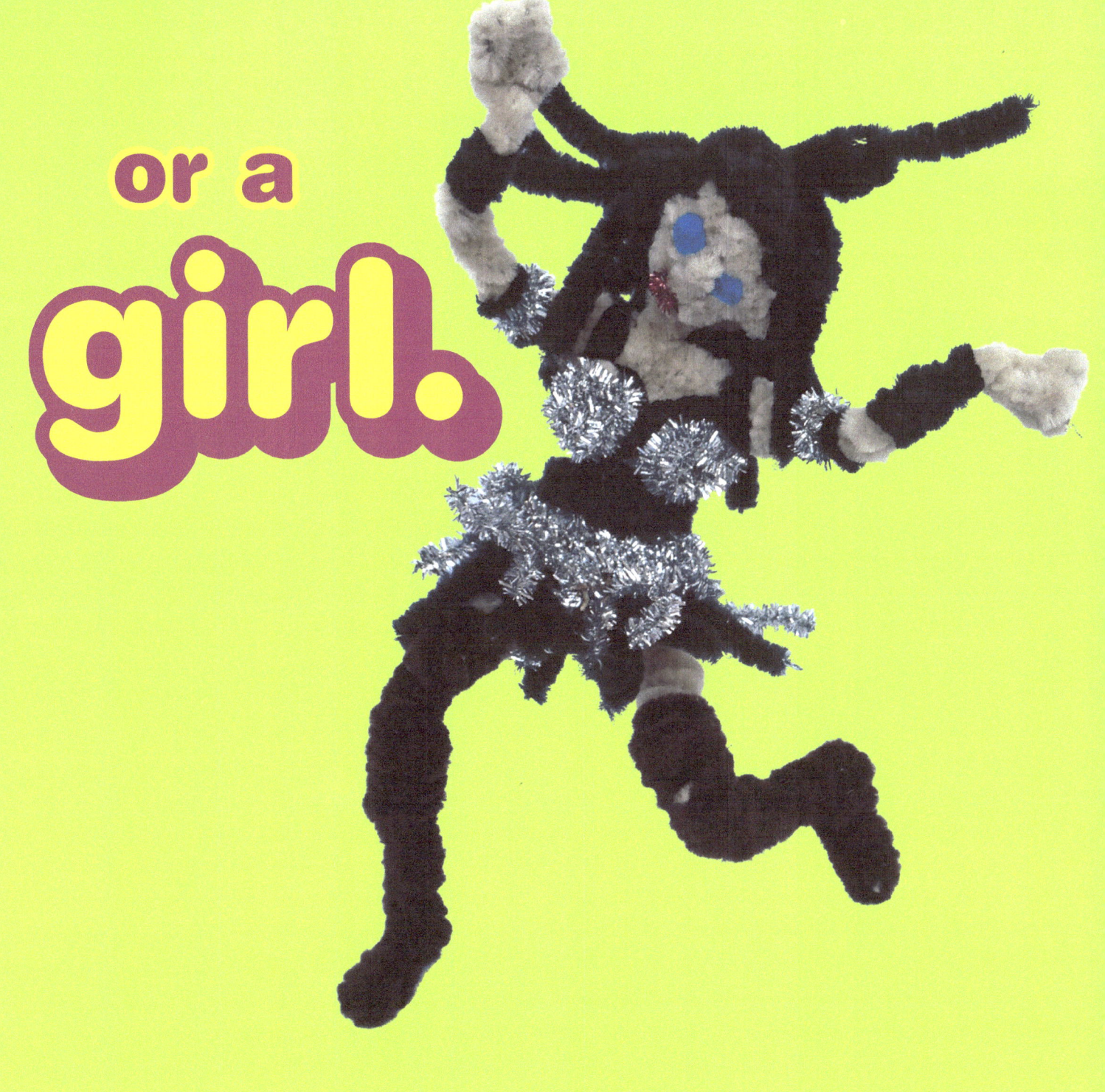

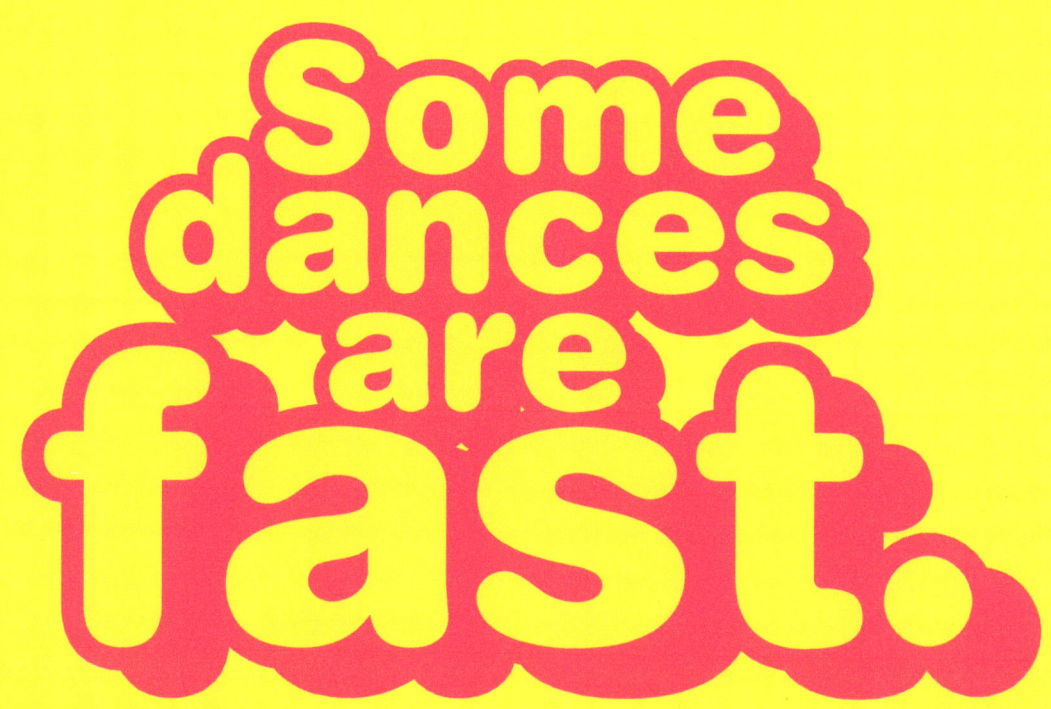

Some dances are slow.

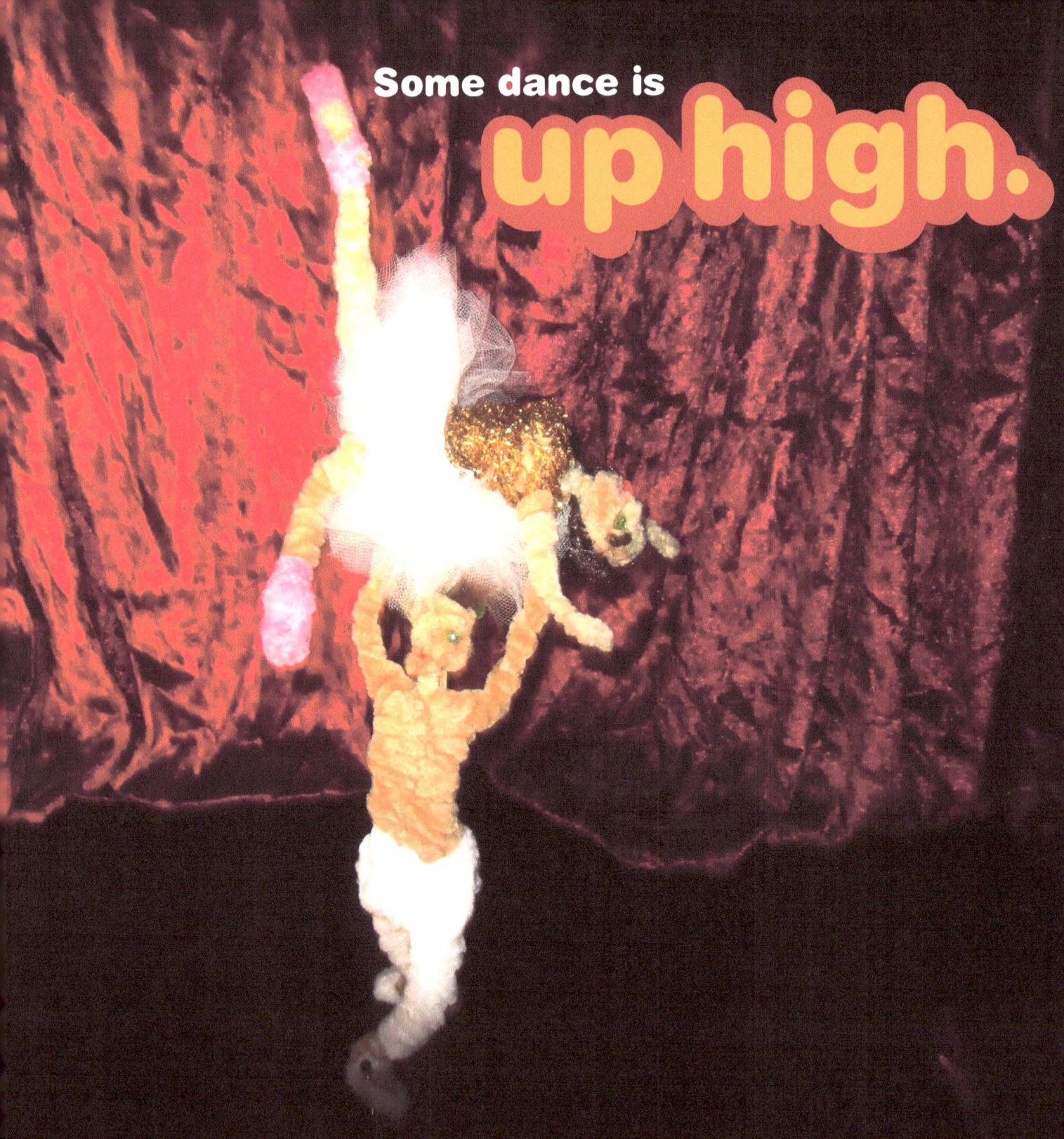

Some dance is **up high.**

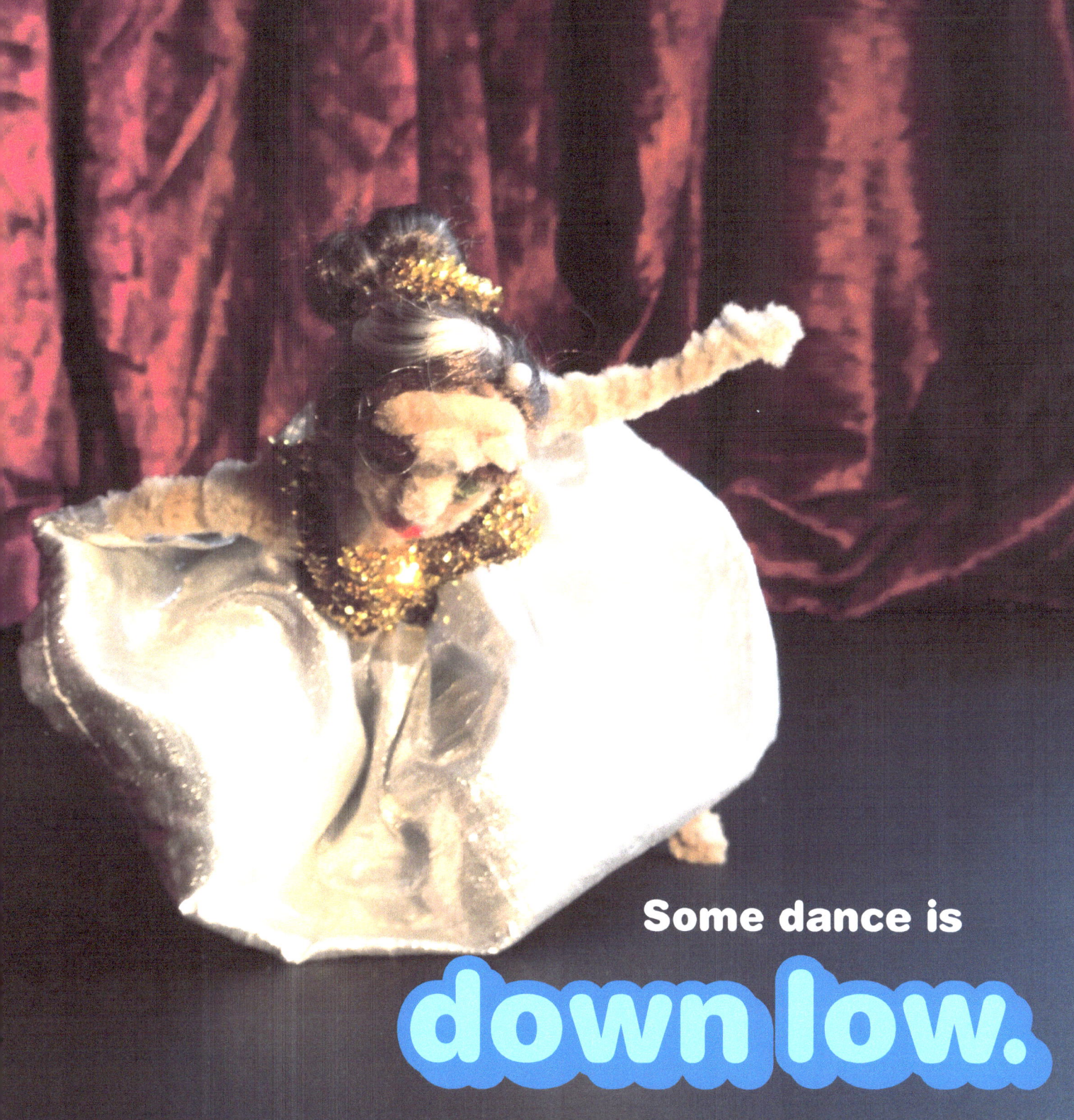

Some dance is
down low.

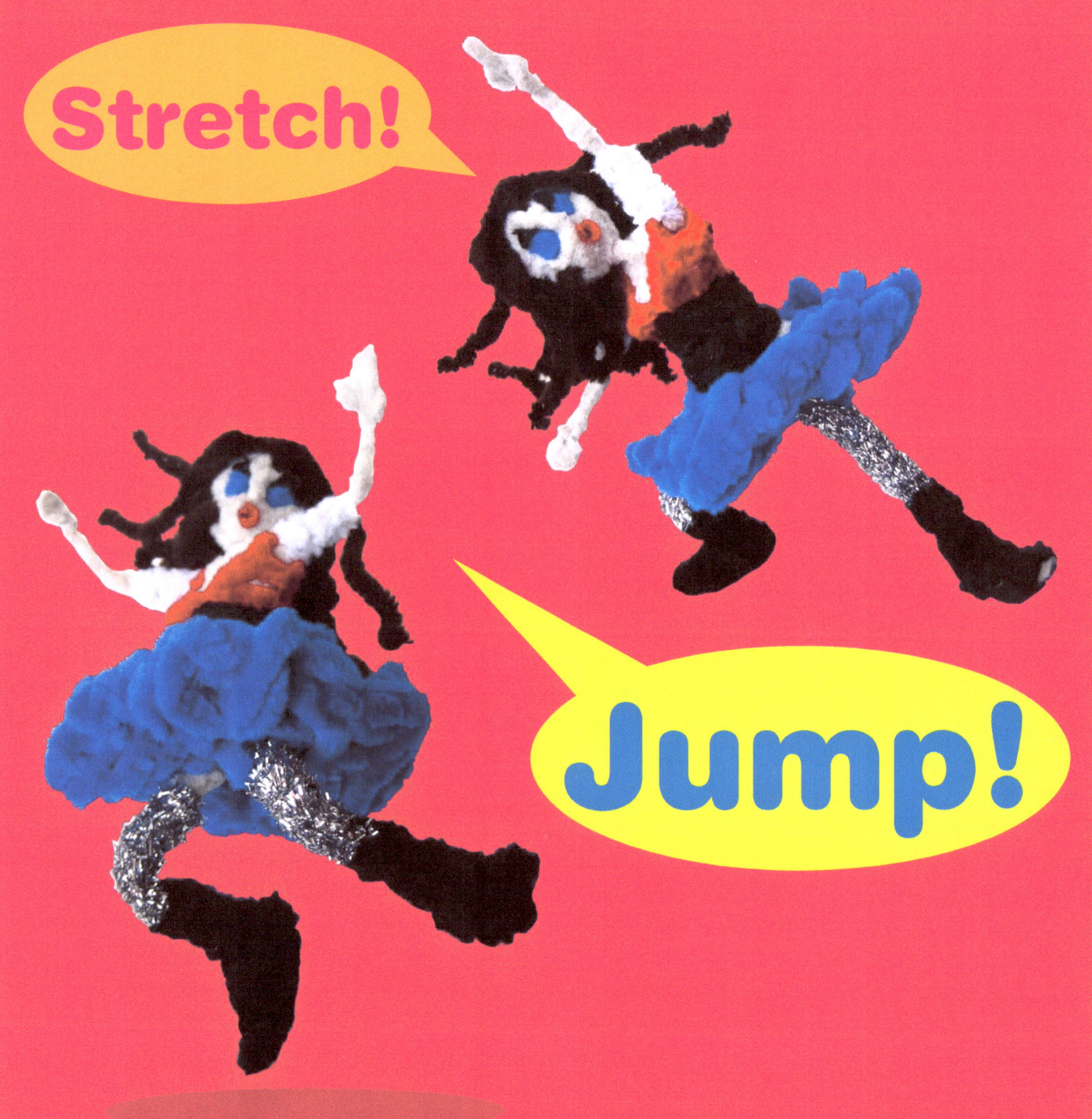

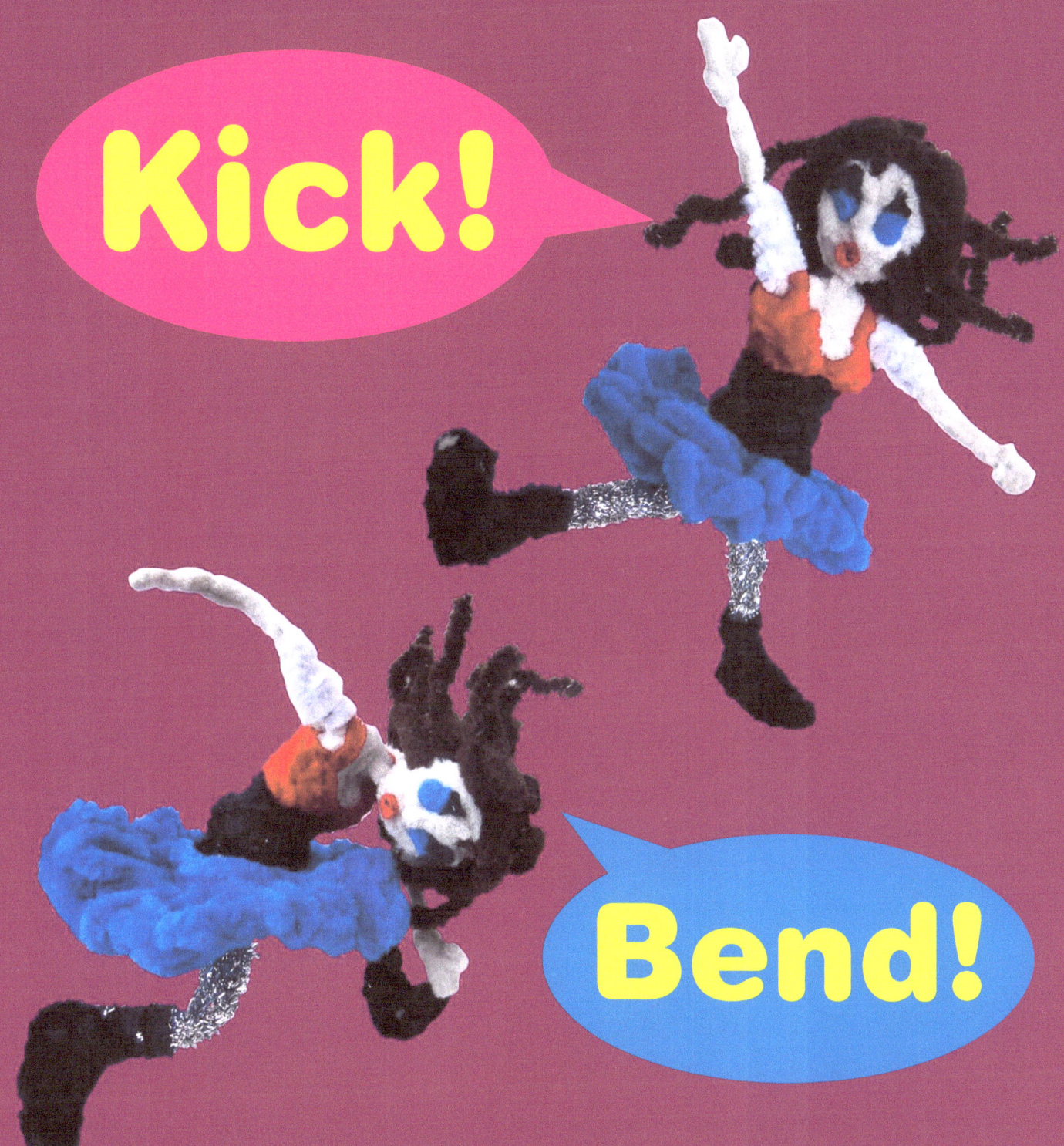

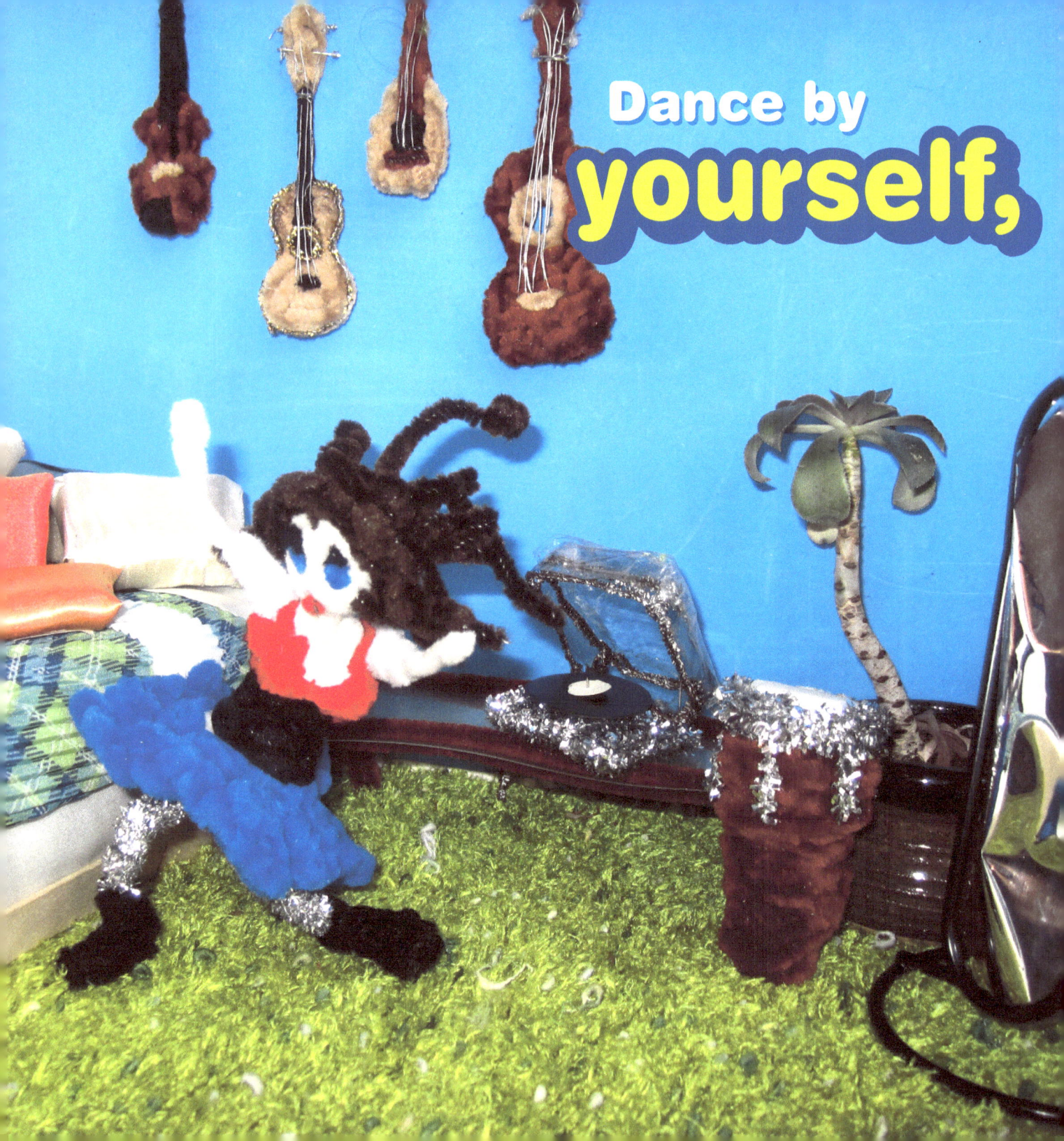

Dance by **yourself,**

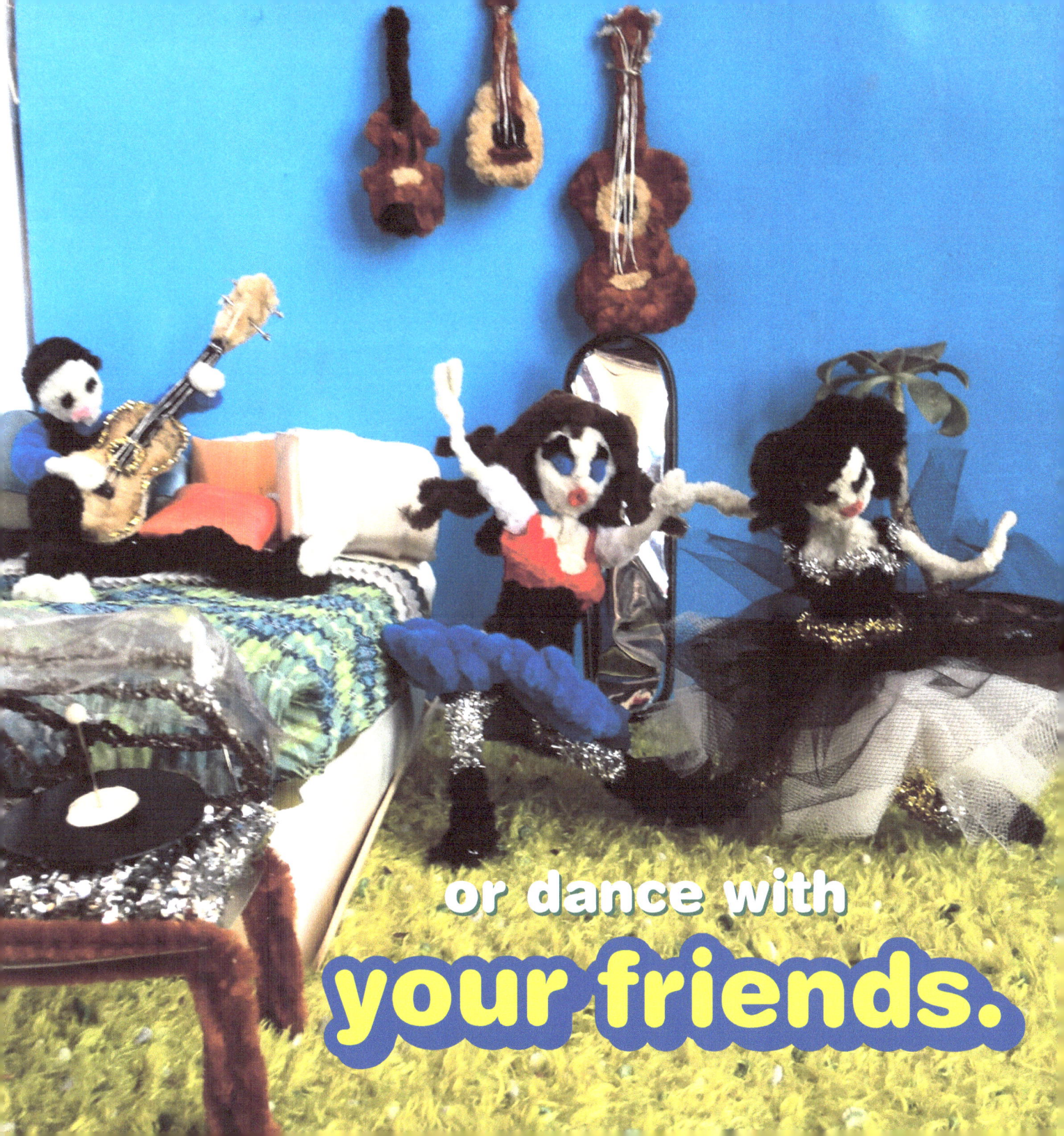

or dance with **your friends.**

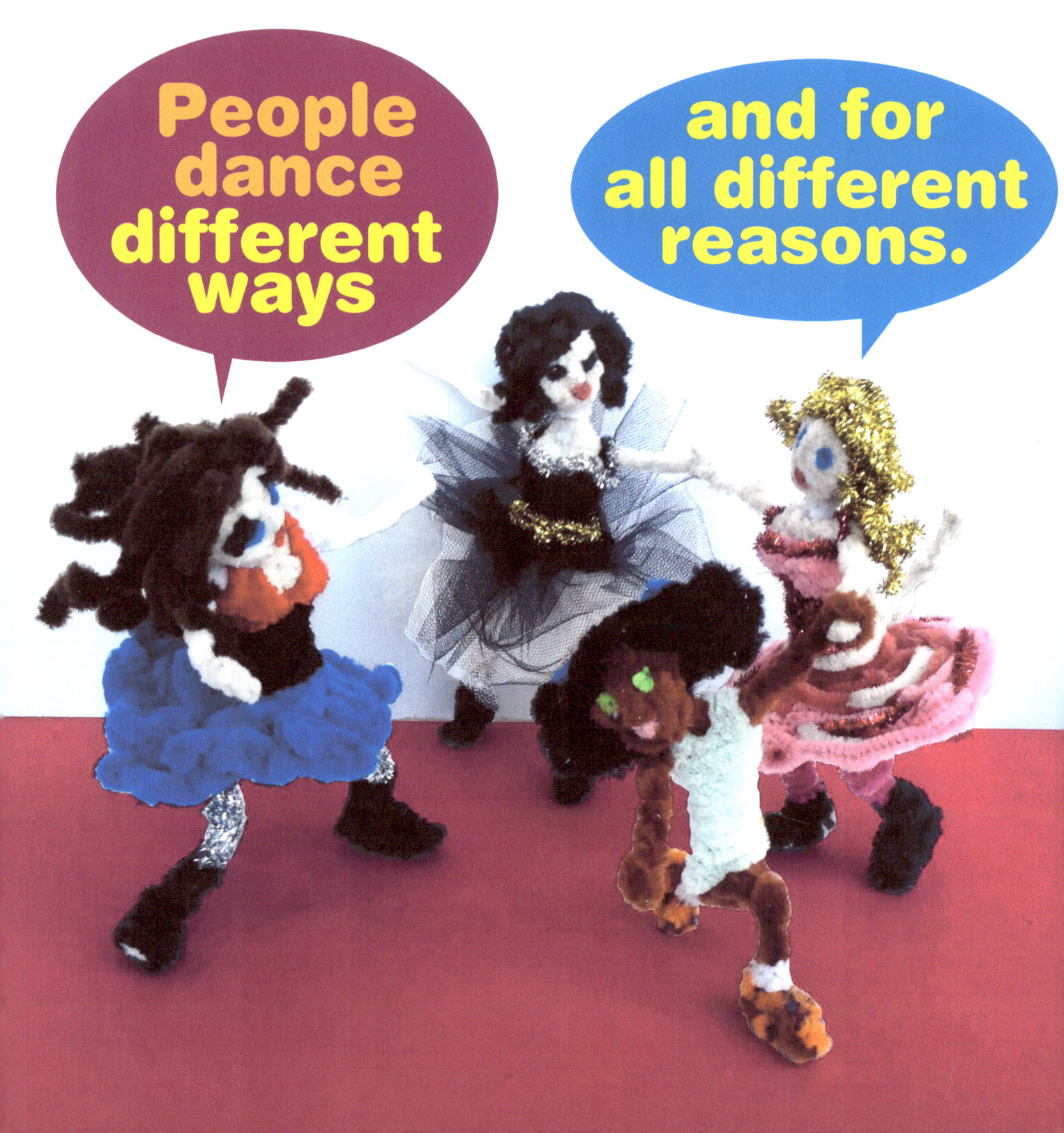

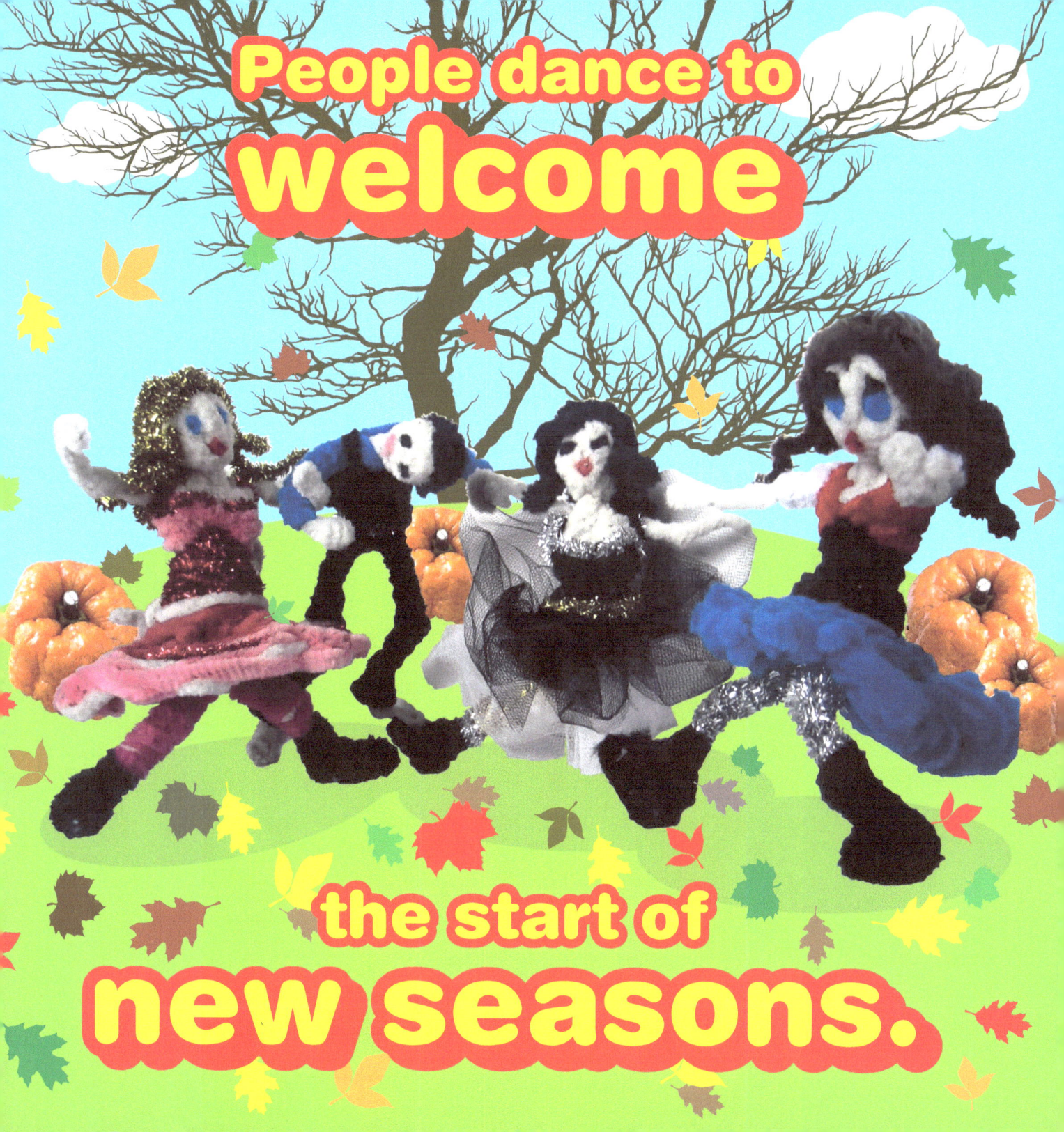

People dance to **welcome**

the start of **new seasons.**

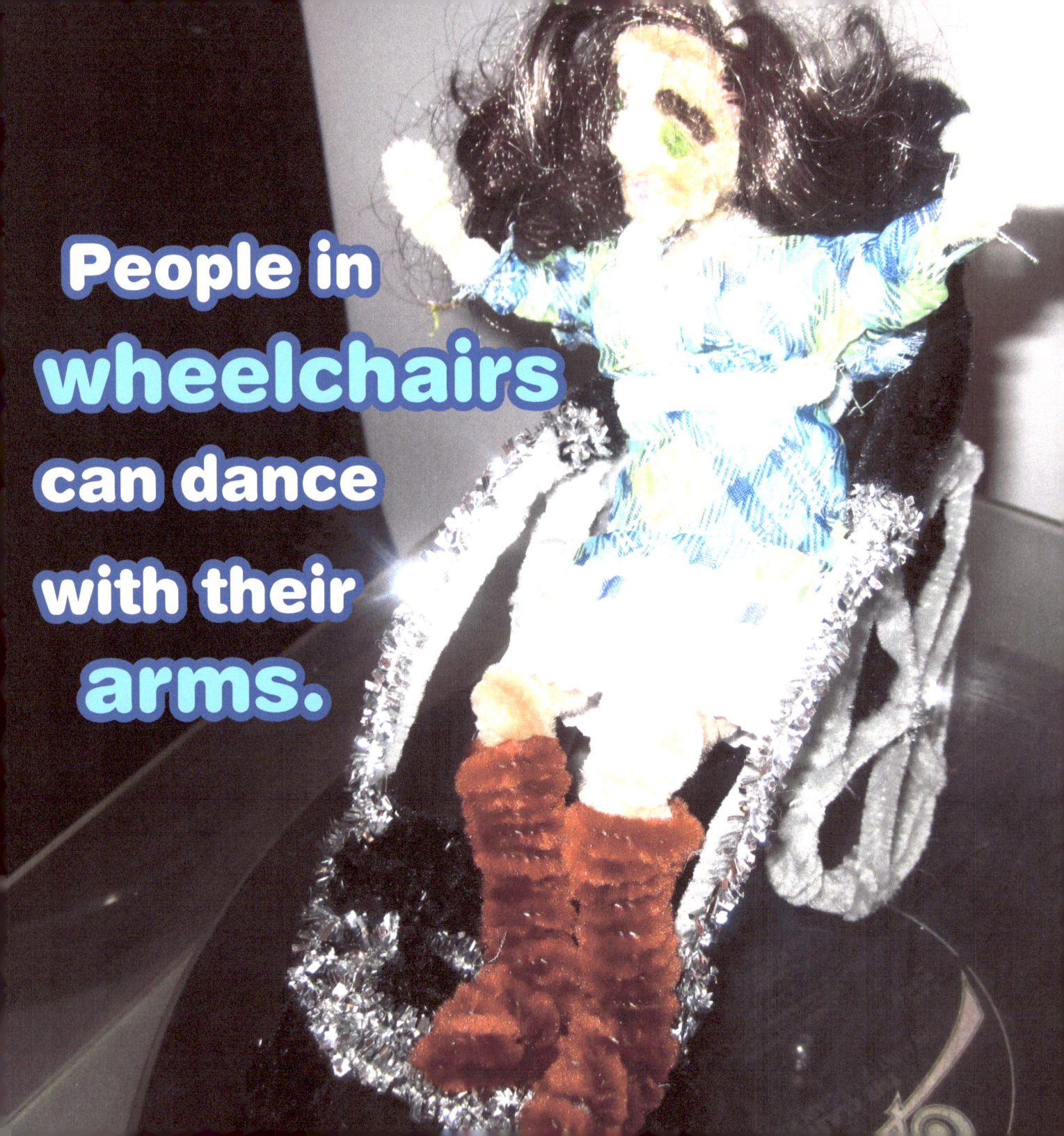

People in **wheelchairs** can dance with their **arms.**

People in traffic can

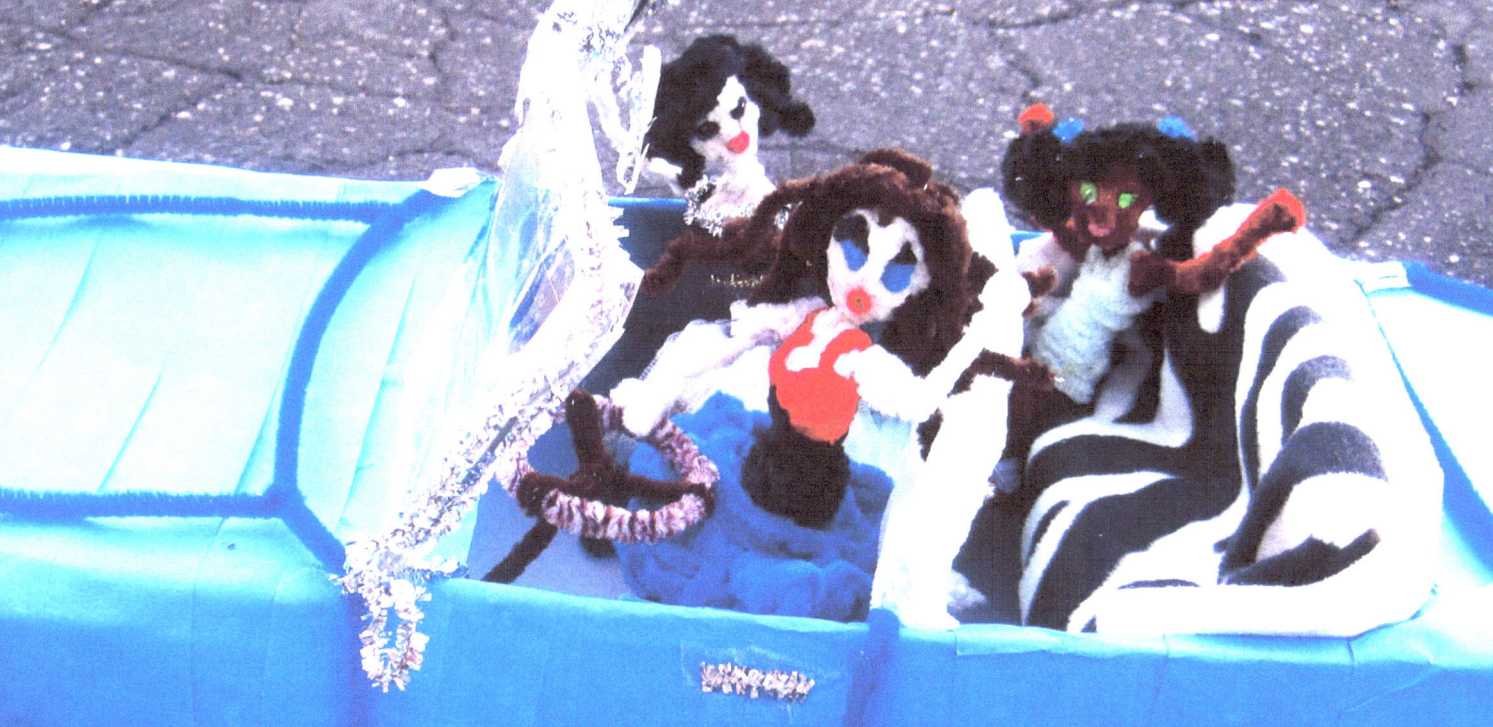

dance in their cars.

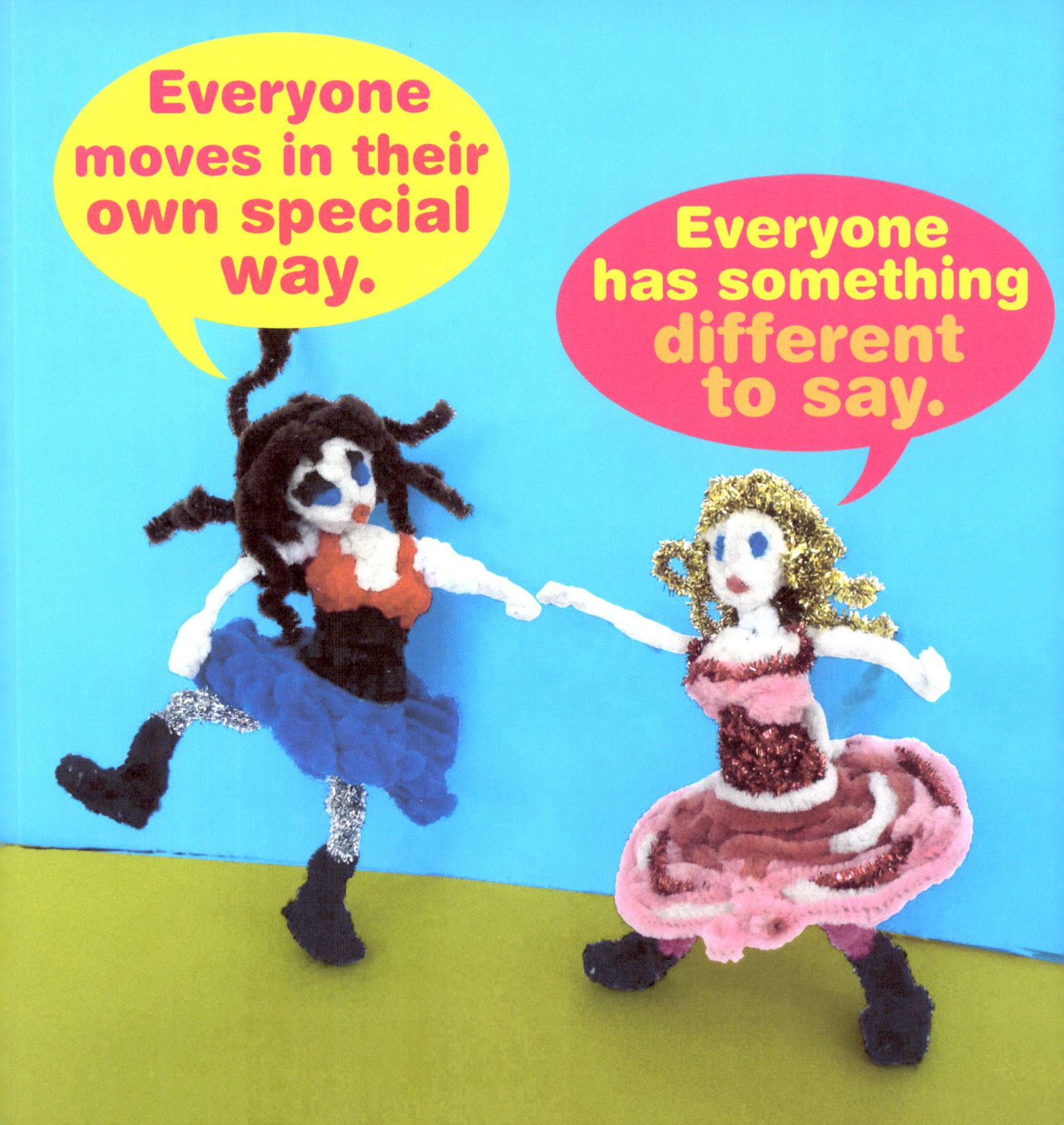

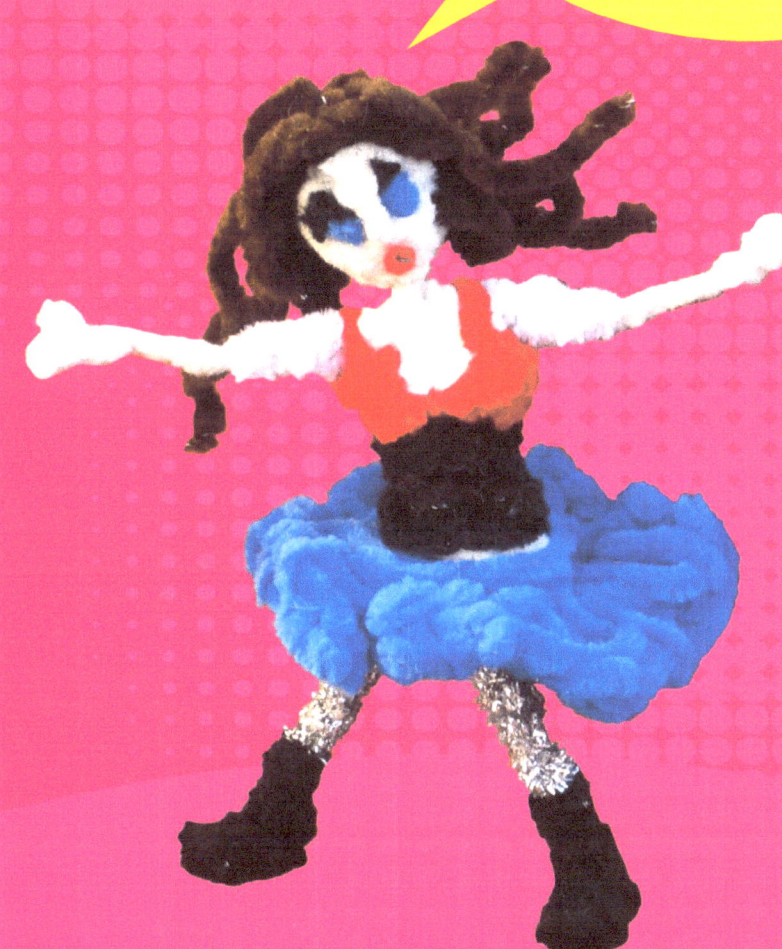

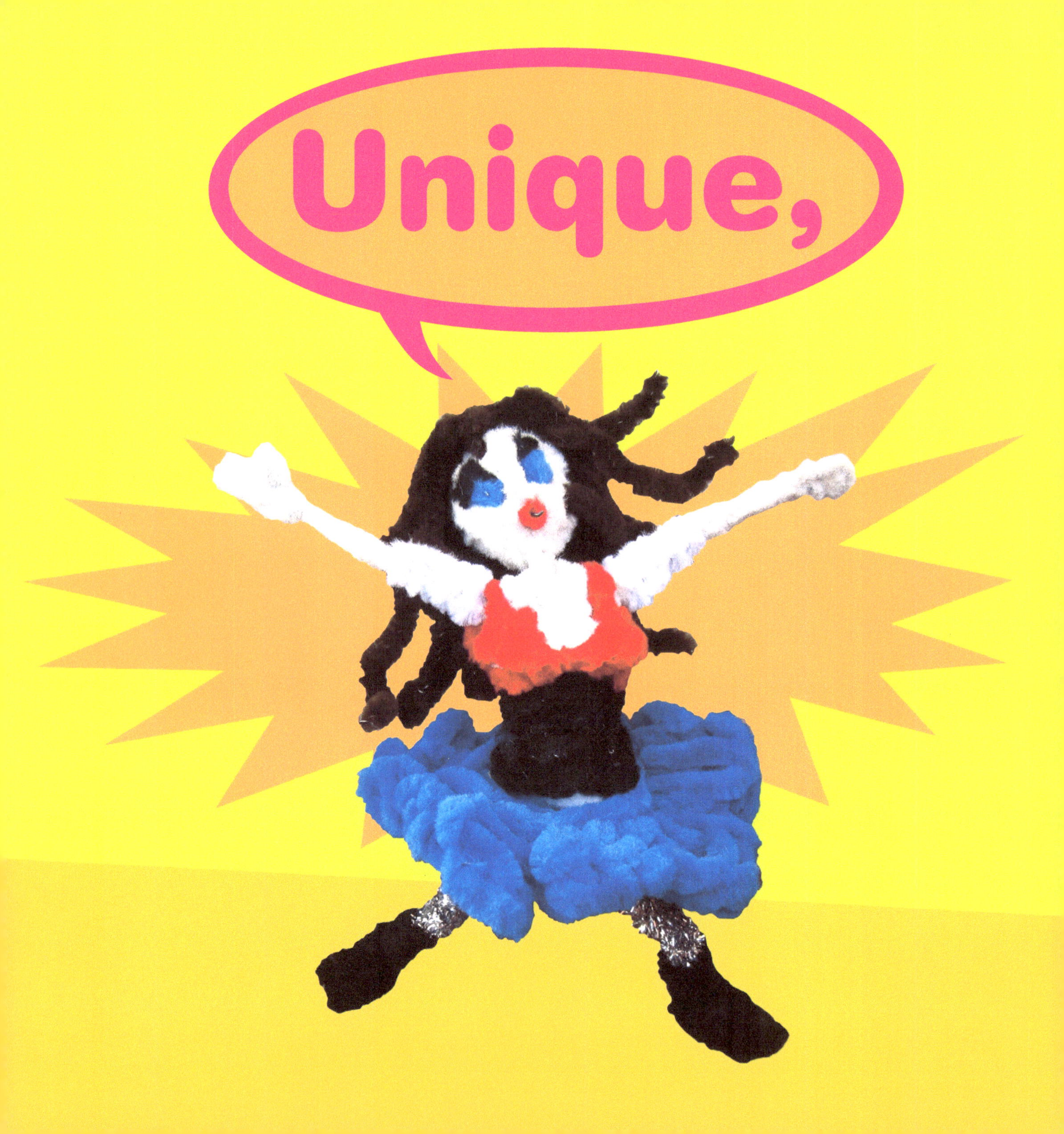

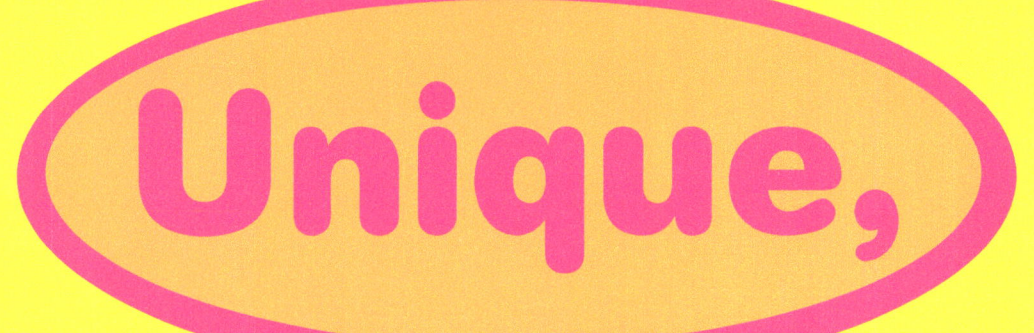

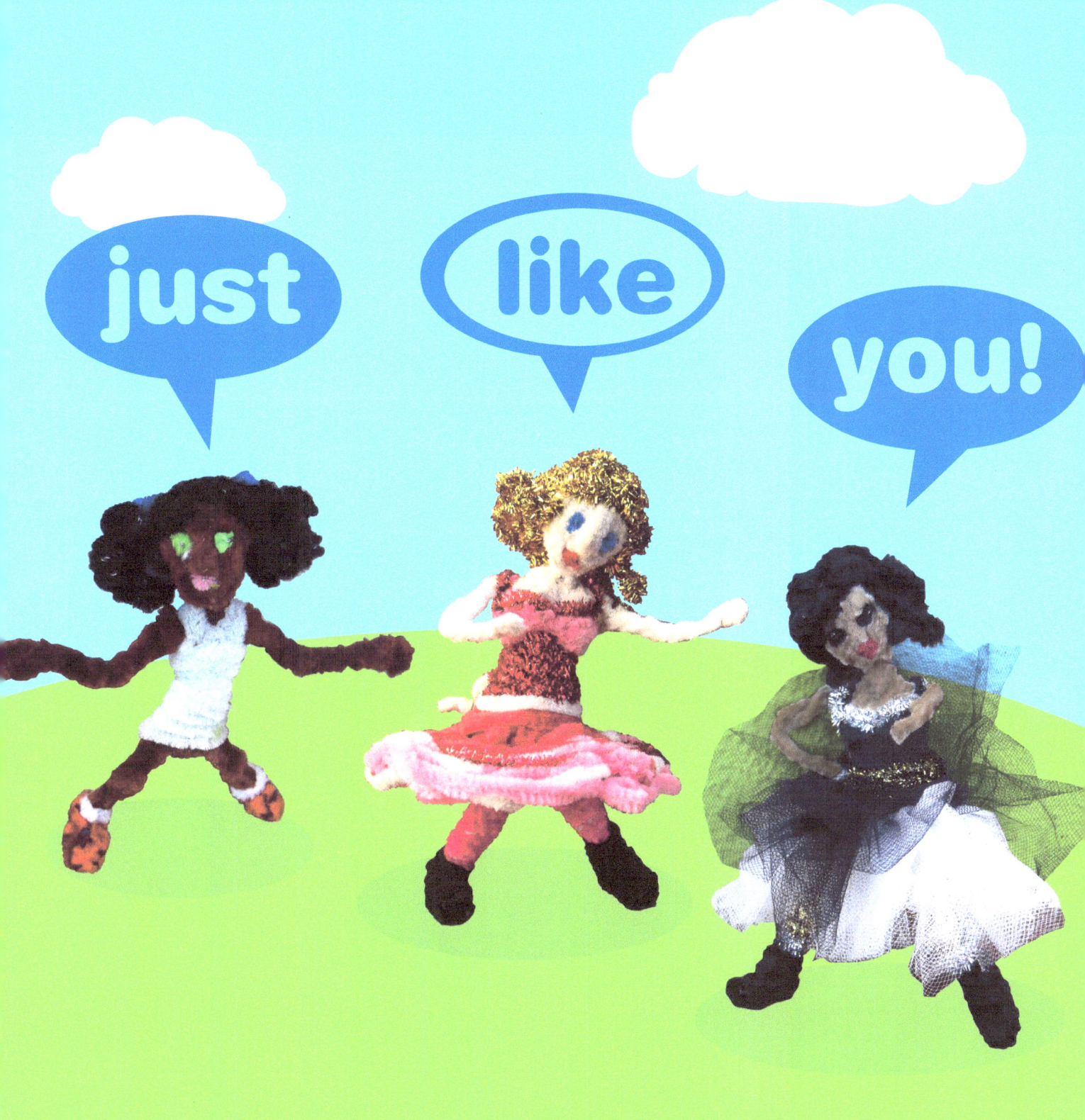

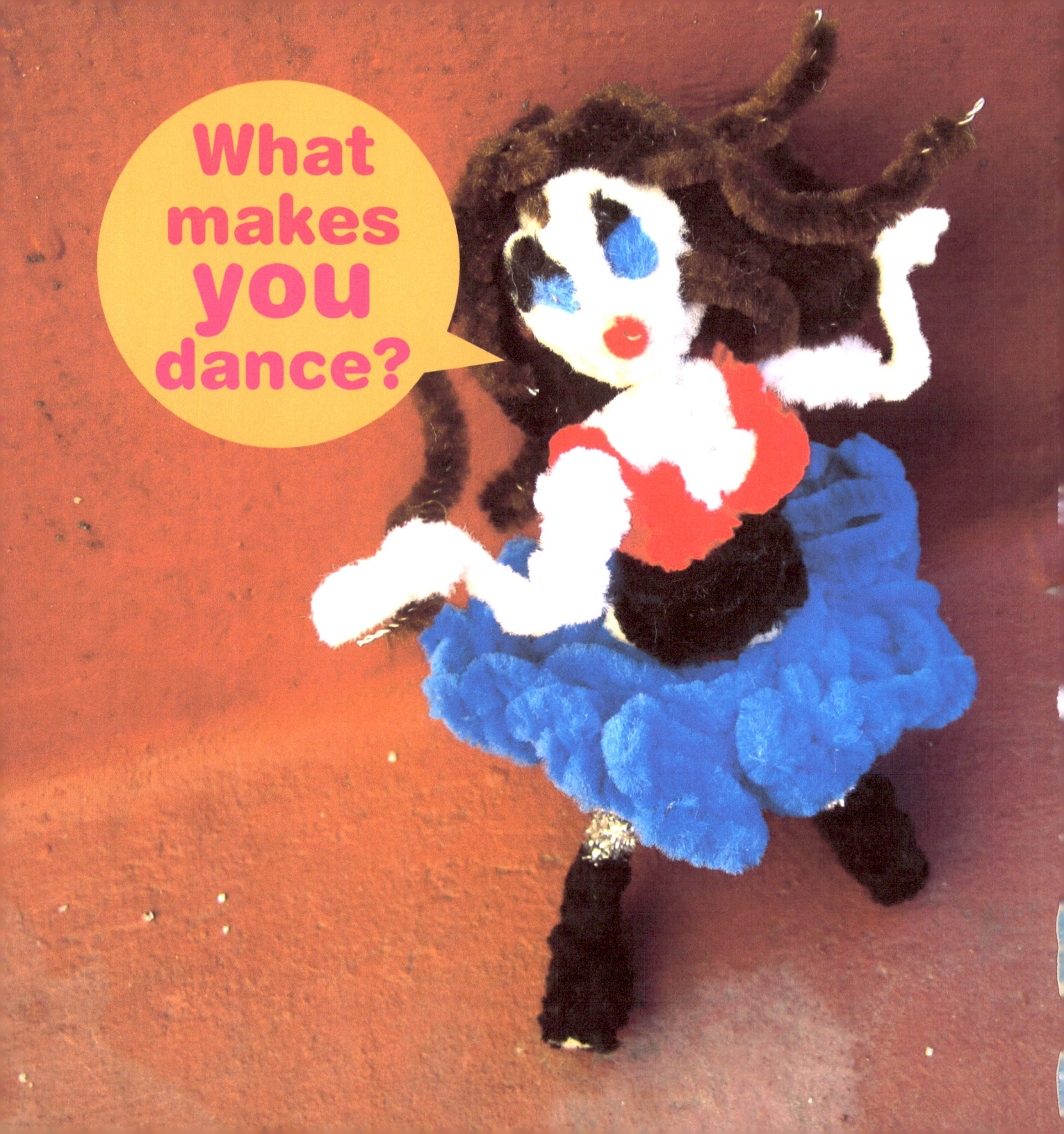

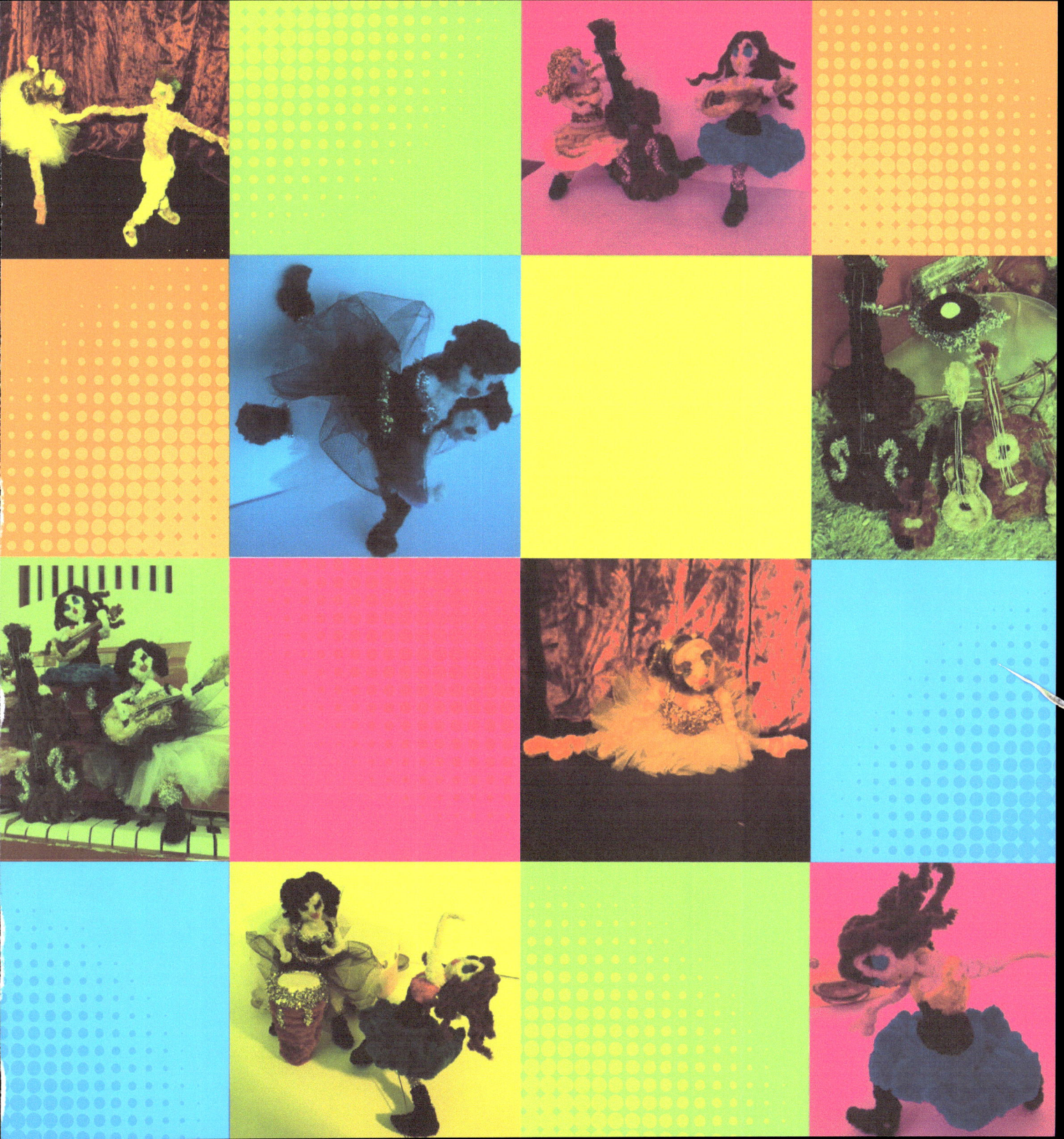

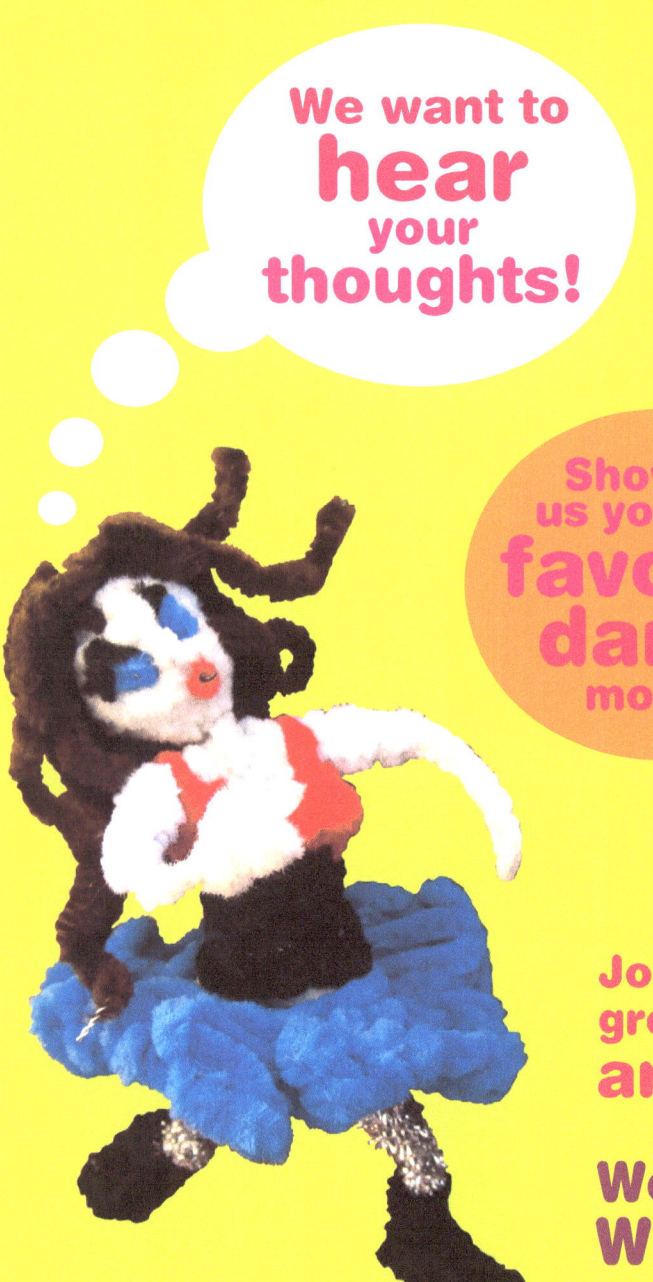